Through Isabella's Eyes

Beth Abbott

ISBN: 978-1-916596-33-7

Contents

Introduction

My name is Beth Abbott, but my close friends call me B. I am in recovery from an alcohol addiction that I had for most of my life. I wanted to create a book that would help others in recovery or active addiction, whether recovering from addiction, mental health, or a toxic relationship. I wanted to give you some tools and advice and tell you some of the things that have helped me in a raw truthful, and authentic way.

I'm just going to get it out of the way now. If you are part of the punctuation police or get offended by swear words or a bit of Brummie slang here and there, this is not the book for you. (Just as a side note, I have Dyslexia and am awaiting an ADHD diagnosis so to sit down and write this was no easy feat let me tell you) If I wrote a lardy dah book sugar-coating over life, then it wouldn't be honest, and it certainly wouldn't be describing the world of addiction, that's for sure. Writing the book was far, far more straightforward than editing it because the editor tool seemed to want to strip it of all its creativity and make it very informal, as though I was sending an email to a CEO.

So, I started rebelling against it a bit in the end in a true addict style, fuck you, I will say, actually and like one million times because I am a Brummie. On that note, true Brummie's spell it MOM, not MUM, and that's final aha.

I've also found out there are other ways I can describe things other than calling everything amazing, words such as fantastic, tremendous, exquisite, fan daby bloody dosey.

I have been sober for three years now, yet I still get drinking dreams most nights.

They used to scare me, but not so much now. In my dream, I am never drinking alcohol, always drunk, wanting desperately to be sober or sober but hung over, desperately craving the hair of the dog. My whole body feels the sensations when I wake up. My dreams always, at some point, bring me back to my childhood home to pure trauma. Maybe it is because I still need healing from these things; the dreams are a stark reminder of that.

Or maybe it's just my addictive mind being an arsehole (it could be both).

I believe that home was full of toxic energy, maybe even evil spirits, my home now with my daughter is full of love, and you can feel it in its energy. My last home, when I lived in a house, ended up with the same hollow energy, and that is because I gave up on wanting to live any more in there. If not for my daughter Isabella or my path to recovery, I would have taken my life there.

That seems like such a bold statement, yet true because I was in so much unbearable pain. There were days I could not breathe through the pain; I just drank through it. That home was a place of addiction and domestic violence because when you add alcohol lots and lots of alcohol into any situation, it will end badly, and it did unbelievably bad.

I lost myself completely. My spirit had left for a while. I was just a shell of who I thought I was, fuelled by only alcohol. My eyes were red and lifeless, and my skin was grey, almost transparent. I loved my daughter, but at the time, my demons had the better of me in that home, I blended into the social dynamics of the area, and I became a product of my environment but the worst product. A real-life Frank Gallagher, only his hair was probably less greasy.

Yet the very demons that sucked from my soul at the time and stole my spirit are the ones that led me to the path of inner peace. (Not that they intended to do so, of course) I do not regret my addiction; I feel remorse for the pain it coursed to those who loved me, especially my sweet innocent baby girl. She is the light of my life, the reason for my existence still on this earth and my proudest achievement.

Although it was the alcohol that nearly killed me in the last home. It was also alcohol that saved me from the reality of the first one. The drink is for escapism. At least it was for me, yet I did not want to drink to be merry and forget.

On many occasions, I wanted to drink to oblivion with the hope I would not wake up. I just want to clarify that I am a million miles away from feeling like that and live a peaceful, contented, authentic life now. If you take the time to read this, you can too. I promise you, you can. My mental health has always been volatile. Hormones, men, family situations, and an overwhelming desire to fill an unfillable void all piled into it until, one day, I just crumbled.

I believe I was having a spiritual, physical, and mental breakdown. I ALSO BELIEVE I NEEDED IT. I am also so incredibly grateful for it. Those darkest days led me eventually to the lighter ones. I had to break before I could mend. It sounds deep, doesn't it, and a little unfair that you must go so deep down the rabbit hole to find the rope at the bottom to pull you up, but with addiction, you kind of have to.

Everybody has different breaking points; some people have ten rock bottoms, each worse than the one before, because, in active addiction, you are always changing the bar and the posts to fit around the lies you tell yourself while the whole time telling yourself you do not have an addiction.

You would think the first time I ended up in the hospital as a teen would have put me off, but it never did. There were about eight more ambulance rides ahead of me. The final one was when the mental health team had to come out to assess whether I needed sectioning because I was suicidal. Sometimes when you went to the hospital, if you got empathetic doctors or nurses, they would put you on a drip to help with the withdrawals, sometimes though they would not, and that night the bed was rattling as I shook.

I smelt like piss because I had heaved so much when throwing up that I wet myself. I didn't, at that point, even care. All I could fixate on was getting out of there and getting some vodka to stop the withdrawals because it felt like if I never got it, I was going to die either way. A couple of months before that, I had been in hospital because I called an ambulance because I was throwing up blood.

It turns out it was just the lining of my throat. Cheap vodka will do that to you. My Dad and little Brother Hen came to get me. It must have just been heart-breaking for them to see me like that, it wasn't a one-off, so the severity of it just seemed to get less and less each time. How can you want to drink something that ends with a hospital visit?

Each time your family gets the call, they don't know whether you have had an accident or attempted to take your life. They must have felt like their lives were held ransom to that phone.

Easy to say now, though, because hindsight is a beautiful thing. Addiction, in the end, felt like everyone else was out to get you, on your case, doing your head in. How can they not see your pain? You do not want to be this person.

You just do not know how to stop. You can't contemplate a world without your crutch. It was your best friend once, now, though. Even though it's your worst enemy, you still crave those days when it soothed you, sent you to sleep like you were on a soft fluffy cloud being sang lullabies.

Even though the lullabies are now loud echoing screams in your head, you can't contemplate the loneliness of not hearing them either. Apart from my love for my daughter or close family, I do not think I knew what pure love was, family and friends, but that's a different kind of love.

I have loved and had many ridiculous male choices along the way. However, my version of love was distorted because my reality was distorted. My emotions amplified with intoxication, so I did not know how I felt about anything for a long time. Do not get me wrong, I thought it was love. It may well have been my version of love, but it is not the kind of love I would invite into my life today.

Today I would say that love is kind. I would say that it is not all those massive gestures you see in the movies but a compromise that is shown via actions, not empty words. It is a scale that can rock back and forth but have an equal average of back and forth.

It is embracing the good times with your partner but riding the waves through the bad ones. Little looks of reassurance and being at peace with each other when the room is silent, putting someone else's needs above your own when their need is higher because true love wouldn't take emotional advantage of another person.

On that note, here is my poem What is love?

What Is Love?

The two most over used words are I love you and I am sorry;
those words go hand in hand but are misused
To bring confusion to the abused
The actions of another can be in fact anything but those three
words
They seem to erase heart ache though when they are heard
Which is crazy because it's the one saying those words that
caused you the hurt in the first place
But It's like you're a vampire who has tried your first bite had
your first blood taste
So, you go back for more
But when the sorry I love you hits you in your core
You forget why you was sad, hurt, angry or upset
But never forget
Your worth, Your self-respect
While you're building up another yourself you forget
I know now love is not something you say it's the things that
you do
But It's a learning curve in this world that feels new
Love is little moments that don't need words or sound
Picking up broken people from the ground
But not reminding them they once were broken
Because Love doesn't like those words being spoken
It's the most beautiful thing in the world but it can crush you in
the wrong hands
You feel as though you are the only one who feels that way and
no one understands
But That's not love its toxic infatuation
That thrives on fights and intoxication
To survive
When it's quiet it's those fights, you crave so you thrive
On the thought of making up
But What goes up must come down
You are the butt of their jokes their juggling clown
That's not love, Love is patient, love is calm, and it is kind
It can be hard to leave the past behind

But as you are evolving and changing so should your
misconceptions
About hurt and rejections
Because What will be will be, love finds its way back through
complications
If only we learnt the art of communication
I am your feather to fly not your anchor to sink and you are hers
or his
That's what Love is

I did not just try to fill the void with Alcohol, drugs, hair extensions, make up, AMAZON, I filled it with men (many men).

Men I knew would not love me, or that they would hurt me almost like in a way to feed into the pain I felt. An excuse for bad behaviour. Sex feels great in that moment, and just like alcohol, though, once it is over, the binge is done, you are just left with another chink in the armour, just another tally on the board.

On the outside, you are promiscuous and a bit of a tart. It may come across that you are full of confidence, but that was the furthest away from the truth you could find. (After a bottle of brandy, though, it was a different story) I have always been an empath and can truly feel other people's pain.

This can be a wonderful thing to have, to have the ability to empathise wholeheartedly with other people's situations. It can also have it is downsides. Like you are a sponge, you absorb all the energy of a room.

Therefore, I find it hard to be in busy places or places with low energy. It does affect me. I would never want to change that side of me, though, because it has helped me to help others, which also gives me feelings of joy. However, being an empath is like a moth to a flame for a narcissist. I was the fuel to many, and as I poured more gas into their motor, mine emptied and finally shut down.

Like a sand glass, you are emptying bit by bit while they feed from your source until there is not even a grain of sand left, and then and only then is when they would be done. A pissed-up girl with low self-esteem and a big heart is pretty much gold dust to a narcissist.

This is not the ex-bashing bit, by the way. I chose these people because, at the time, I believed that was all I deserved. You can become more addicted to a person than any drink or drug, I believe. The highs, and the lows, I quite liked feeling the pain.

There was a comfort in it. The nasty words that would be said confirmed everything I believed about myself. Just like at the beginning, alcohol took me away from my first house, men filled the emptiness, if only for a second or so.

That is until I was left with a bigger dent than the one there before. Everyone you sleep with is like giving away a little part of yourself. I don't know the names of some, wouldn't know their faces, yet they have been inside my body.

That seems so appalling coming from a woman, but would it be looked upon with so much disgust if a man wrote this book?

That would be a high-five moment I recon every holes a goal and all that.

In the sober cold light of day, that's a haunting thought. In fairness, though most of these years are a bit of a blur, alcohol is the social lubricant of life, and sex makes you feel desired synthetic confidence that doesn't exist. A bit like ballroom Cinderella vanishes when the clock runs out; that's us when the buzz runs out.

Dragon Girl

There once was a flickering flame this girl was wild and free
You could see the candlelight it burned bright for all to see
Once there was a girl who turned into a dragon
Then eve fell in love with Adam
The fire should have been fuelled more
But it turned to ashes on the floor
He didn't want that flame to burn at least not that bright
So, he'd whisper nasty things until she froze at night
While you're sleeping warrior, I'll take this battle for you
While you freeze from a frozen heart while your heart is blue
I'll light a fire child, I'll let it heat you up
Sleep little dragon girl I won't interrupt
Oh, little dragon girl you will find your fire again
It will burn twice as hot it will burn through your pain
So little dragon girl sleep for a while
Until you wake with happy thoughts until you wake and smile

Chapter One

The Number 15

So, we just chase increasingly till the pumpkin explodes, and the illusion is seen no longer to be accurate. I'm not that person anymore, and I haven't been that person for a very long time. I love my partner now.

I never ask him about his past. He never asked me about mine because before we met, anything we did then was irrelevant to our relationship. Of course, we know bits and pieces, but I would never ask him numbers or anything like that because I just don't care. What matters is the here and now.

The number fifteen has always stood out to me. That is because that is when I lost my innocence. Experts say addiction keeps you in the same mindset as when you first started it. I was thirty-one when I first went into rehab, Yet I felt fifteen.

I had a child, a house, and an excellent job, although I burnt many bridges with jobs over the years with Monday excuses. I felt like I was on autopilot mode, like it wasn't my life that this was happening too. I spent most of my life supporting others.

Yet there I was, broken, scared, full of bitterness and resentment, ashamed, and unbearably full of guilt. If I am honest, I wanted nothing more when I first entered recovery than to just drink all the vodka in the world. A fountain of it, Niagara Falls would not have felt like enough.

When someone tells you, you cannot do something, you want to do it ten times more. Like a toddler not getting its way, the addicted part of your brain has one last tantrum trying to get its way. I can look at alcohol bottles behind the counter now, I can see them and know that they will not hurt me.

I do not have to whisper half a bottle of glens to the cashier at 8.30 in the morning just to take what I call the heaby jeabies away. As I am writing this, I am thinking, 'shut the fuck up; no one cares. Stop trying to be something you are not your poetries shit, who even likes poetry any way blah bablah' Even in recovery, my head still attacks me daily. It gets a little quieter each day if I am doing what I should be doing!

Even that's not enough, though. I have brought rose quarts for self-love and sagged my house to eliminate toxic energies. I will try anything. Recovery is about being open to learning new things and being teachable.

This is not me pushing my beliefs onto you, either. Whatever works for you is all that matters. The meaning of the word god can come in lots of different forms. The simple things, though, like not showing gratitude or holding on to resentments, will take you out the door.

Although I try to practice these things, I still have days where I feel low or cannot seem to find the ability to find gratitude. Even though I am so far away from where I was, I am nowhere near where I want to be, and I am so ridiculously hard on myself for that. I am on doctor's medication for depression, anxiety, and a few other things, which is ok. I am not ashamed of that.

I am not writing this for sympathy or to make it all about me and my mental health struggles, which I worry about as I write. I am authoring this book for someone to relate, and to talk about some of the things that have helped me along the way.

I want to put in a few relevant poems here and there. I have been so incredibly fortunate, I have always had my poetry to turn to, and it has always been such a passion of mine, which is now part of my community interest company too, which just goes to show if you have a passion, you can turn it into a career.

It would be an honour and privilege to be part of the process of helping others to heal. Writing these words down for this book is healing my soul if I am truthful. It truly is so much better out than in. I advise so many people to do things, yet ironically, I can forget to do them for myself.

I guess we can all do that at times. My head gets busy, and life takes over. I have moments when walking down the road when it feels like I have an out-of-body experience. It's like it is me but not me (just to clarify, I have not replaced the alcohol with mushrooms or acid). Sometimes, I like to break myself down into pieces.

I wrote a poem about it called...

The Many Masks We Wear

The many faces we wear, each one a different mask
Which one is truly you as you pick them for each task?
A mask for a mother a mask for a friend
A mask thrown away when it's reached the end
A mask for a business owner to show authority
A mask full of makeup to hide insecurity
A mask when you're learning open to innovative ideas
A mask to show courage to hide your fears
A mask when your glammed up for a night out
A mask of assertiveness to hide your doubt
A mask you put on when you're feeling defensive
There's so many to choose so which ones authentic?
Was a mask not worn with hair upon your head?
When you take them all off when you are lying in bed
Which mask must you place on your face today?
To take on the many roles that we must play

The whole purpose of this poem is I am a completely different version of myself dolled up with war paint on than I am sitting in my PJs with Sudo cream on my face. We must be so many different versions of ourselves we never stop to think and ask ourselves who we are?

I decided to write down all the different versions of myself I must try and be.

Try to imagine you put a battery percentage next to it. Which one consumes the most energy?

Is energy used well, or could it be used more productively on other things?

When I was in active addiction, I'd roll out of bed like the Tasmanian devil and leave everything to the last minute. The school-run version of me was a fucking flaming ball of a hot mess.

I decided that today's version of myself would start being kinder to tomorrow's version. All a bit pretentious and Lardy dah, but it can be simple things like preparing the uniform, washing the dishes, and putting the bloody school shoes somewhere where I can find them.

Them bastards always disappear just as you are about to leave the door, well, at least, they used to. I wake up an hour earlier, play some music have a fag, sorry not quite quit that filthy habit yet, but I will though when I am ready.

We do not skip out of here like the Waltons in the morning. Sometimes, I even want to head butt my drywall when it takes her 10 mins to put a single sock on, but it is better, much better.

I saw this saying once it said, 'drinking today is like stealing a little bit of your happiness from tomorrow,' and it stuck. I do not mean for the so-called weekend social drinkers who are drinking to have fun. The hangover is worth it if you have stopped drinking to oblivion and it was a Friday night, so technically, you can spend Saturday slobbing in bed.

I mean for the addict who drank every day and increasingly as the disease progressed, we stole happiness from every tomorrow, and we regretted most of the yesterdays.

I'm going to Add a poem now I wrote in 2010, my daughter was merely a twinkle in my eye, and I had no clue I'd become a girl who sat in meetings having to introduce myself as an alcoholic before I could speak.

The poem is just really about the Monday-to-Friday cycle most of the country is stuck in. It is a cycle that is ingrained in most people, and not drinking alcohol on a Friday and Saturday night, people kind of just treat you like you have a disability, even if it's nothing to do with addiction because you do not drink.

However, you are a bit of a scumbag if you drink on Monday morning. Same with the weather. If you see someone walking down the road with a can on a boiling hot day, you wouldn't think twice about it.

Now if it was raining, you would think they had serious issues. I see many of my friends who haven't got an addiction locked in this cycle, and I can understand why. It's all we have ever known. We are almost conditioned into it a bit, like if you look at the systems of schools or the 9 till 5 jobs.

If we comply with work all week, we can treat ourselves to drink on the weekend, then get back to the graft on Monday. That's not how addiction works, though. The word Friday means nothing to an addict in addiction. Err, ok, that's a lie. We can consume considerably more than we did on a Monday without people getting suspicious. It does not start like that, though. It starts with a midweek Wednesday drink to break up the working week, then slips into Monday to Sunday. I was a functioning alcoholic for an awfully long time without even realising I was.

I was a lot better at hiding it then too. I used to get paid on a Wednesday, so that's when the drinking would start. It was weekly, so by Monday, I had run out of money anyway, so I would have the Monday and Tuesday where I wouldn't touch a drop a bit of a reset.

But eventually, it was just every day. Looking at the clock at first just waiting till it hit a reasonable hour, after the school run when we were settled after tea.

Ultimately, in the end it was after the school run but not the night-time one, the morning one, only if I had a real skinful the night before. I will never forget the shame it used to make me feel. I would wait until the shop was empty after the other moms got bread, milk, and other normal things.

Then I would potter about picking up a few things I didn't need so the emphasis was not on the drink, then I'd make up an excuse like 'I might as well get it now for later' I could spot an alcoholic in a crowd a mile off now, I know every single trick in the book.

I saw a lady once dressed very posh in Bridgnorth, and she was buying Bacardi in the morning. She was telling the cashier how it was a present for someone and getting all flustered (she overexplained). That's what we do.

The sad thing is the cashier doesn't give a shit, you are not the first person that day buying a morning top-up, but we do, so we over-explain it. You can get your drink delivered straight to your door these days, so you haven't even got to deal with those awkward interactions.

That's dangerous. We Isolate in addiction, and now people have not even got to leave the house to go to the shop. Saying that, though, where I lived in Kingshurst in Birmingham, it would be a lot more common than in Bridgnorth.

Although there is a woman I have seen, she just looks so sad. I see the desperation on her face when she is counting her change. I smell that smell of not just alcohol but everything else that goes with it. It's a smell that is hard to explain.

Reused alcohol is a bit like the smell of a carpet in an old pub that just sits on your skin, like it is a layer of you. I once saw that her card had been declined. She had bought cat food with her change first, so she ensured the cat was fed.

I saw her face, and my heart broke. I repeatedly battled with myself in that shop, but I gave her the money to get the bottle. I knew she was not getting help any time soon, but I also knew how ill she would be if she never had it. I did not want to be an enabler and wouldn't make it a habit. I've done that rattle, though, and she could have died.

I saw it in her face I knew how ill she would be. She looked at me, and she cried. I knew it wasn't the right time to talk to her about recovery and rehab. Sometimes you just have to do the kindest thing you can at that moment, even if it makes you feel like a hypocrite full of contradictions.

The Cycle

Friday comes a tot-filled glass
Boobs are out I'm oozing class
I'm too drunk to notice my flat getting trashed
I'm too concerned with getting mashed
Look in the mirror opposite to fit
I'll have a drink do my face in a bit
Sunday comes I'm not so chilled out
I'm delicate so please don't shout
My nose is blocked the worse it's ever felt
I'm roasting and sweating starting to melt
Monday comes and work is dawning
I'm paralyzed in bed still snoring
What excuse can I say they're all getting boring
I can hear the job centre calling
Tuesday comes got to face work
I'm still delicate my head still hurts
Drugs and alcohol can't see the perks
None of these pain killers ever work
Wednesday arrives anxiety attacks have stopped
But I'm still starring at the clock
Just gathering money for the pot
The weekends nearing and I'll spend the lot
Thursdays here Wednesday whizzed past
How long will this meeting last?
I can't be bothered to do that task
Cause Fridays almost in my grasp
Yes, you have guessed its Friday again
I've forgot all about my Monday pain
I'm totted up I've lost my shame
Alcohols being poured like winters rain

Chapter Two

Sayings, quotes, poems, and people

I was vacuuming my rug earlier, and I suddenly remembered when I was poorly. I was at my Aunties place following whatever disaster had happened that week. When I was at my Auntie's, it was my safe place. She filled my heart with so much love I would regress back into a child, lying on her rug for hours in the foetal position like a cat.

There I didn't have to be a woman who worked, a mother, someone who pays the bills, a daughter who disappoints, a sister who brings shame, a friend who embarrasses, or an alcoholic attention seeker.

There I could be a 30-year-old woman lying on the floor in the foetal position, wanting that rug to swallow me up or wrap itself around me like bubble wrap.

My Thirtieth Birthday was a dreadful day. I always hated my birthdays since childhood, so I told myself something terrible would happen yearly.

I moved away when I was sixteen and lived in a hostel, then fell in love with the lad in the hostel down the road, ewe cringe, anyhow, but surprisingly enough, that never worked out. I know, right, shock face. Anyhow, I returned home and ended up in the hostel system just in time for my eighteenth Birthday. 'I am an adult now; nothing can stop me,' eighteen-year-old, but let's go back to becoming thirty years old.

I had people coming around, but I was on the floor in mine by the time they arrived. Not my aunties' soft, safe rug but the hard laminate floor.

I was hysterical when I would drink. It was like a demon was trying to escape my body, I would wail in pain, and the tears would relentlessly fall.

I felt like my life was over, it went down very badly, and once again, I was considered selfish, which I was. Addiction made me selfish all I could feel was my own pain.

My aunty took me back to hers for hours. I cried like a child a lost little child. I wrote this poem once, and it sums up how I felt then and what addiction is. I have it tattooed on my thigh now, too, so it's a reminder of how far I have come but how it feels to be there, and how much I do not want to go back.

The Cold

Warm me up, for I am cold
I started shaking when my soul got sold
Wrap me in a blanket and hide me from this world
For although I have a woman's body, I am just a little girl
Hold out your arms and place my heart within your hand
For you are the one my soul got sold to, so only you can
understand

At the time, I was going through a horrible breakup. At the time, I thought this person was the love of my life. He was the distorted love of my life that version of me anyway. I can't now start denying how I felt then because it felt like love. I know now it was every other emotion but love, because, as I said, I did not know what love was.

There had been many men, flings and infatuations, and many intoxicated fumbles during my addiction, but he stole my spirit and entered my veins, head, heart, and soul.

It was toxic. It was painful. It was an unhealthy level of love.

It was exactly what I wanted at the time because it was exactly how I felt about myself. Every painful word said, or action he did took me deeper into self-sabotage and self-loathing. He was my Kryptonite.

I could not keep away from him; however weak he made me.

However, I would imagine being with me at the time was not a bed of roses either. I was intense, and I revolved alcohol around everything we did.

I would start arguments or get fixations when drunk, usually about someone he had cheated on me with a year ago. In this game of chess, we started playing with each other. Like a chess board, you hurt me, I hurt you, and so the cycle continues.

This version of me today wouldn't put up with the stuff he did to me, and I certainly wouldn't do the stuff I did to him either, or to anyone else or forgive the things I then overlooked.

I read a saying once, hurt people, hurt people.

He is hurting too, but he is on a different journey from me. Maybe he will find peace one day, but I'm sure there will be many broken hearts along the way.

I carried on seeing him for much longer than I should have and lost many family members and friends over it. I would lie to them because I was ashamed.

Ashamed that I still loved, or so I thought, someone who thought so little of me.

They would always find out, though, I was never any good at lying about it, or I would get drunk, and it would all come out.

I wanted to help him even in recovery because I believed there was a good person inside.

Some of me still thinks there is, but that's none of my business anymore. I actually wish him well, though, as insane as that may sound. I have my peace now. It would be nice to think one day he will find his.

However, this book isn't about him; I will leave that there. I just thought it might help someone relate.

Addicts do not do things by halves. They crave all that is bad. If there was a sign on a two-way pathway, one saying DANGER and the other saying contentment, maybe even unicorns, we would end up in the dark forest.

We had all the intentions in the world to go to the candy land of bliss, and we may have even, on a sober day, drawn a map of how to get there.

Then addiction, obsession, compulsive actions, and self-doubt took over.

Then before we knew it, we were tying up our trainer laces and sprinting to the off-license early doors to whisper to the shopkeeper. 'Half a glens, please' like if you whisper to the shopkeeper quickly and hide in your handbag, it does not happen.

Let's face it, that shopkeeper knows you will be back in a couple of hours, not whispering but bold and brash, then again just before closing, stumbling, and slurring.

While candy land awaits your arrival, you have spent your day bottle-watching.

Wondering what emotional river, the clear crack water, will take you on today, who you may offend because they pissed you off three years ago.

Addicts hold on to grudges not when they are sober but when they drink, they get annoyed and bitter over the strangest things.

When all is said and done, all that anger, bitterness, and resentment is internal, and how we feel about ourselves and our cycle. It's far easier to project, which makes you the victim. That way gives another reason to drink.

I liked fire. I had a house at the time with a fire pit in the garden, it was my old neighbour Donna's, but I never gave it back to her.

She must have thought what a liberty every time she saw it smoking, thinking back to it. I brought a mermaid outfit one year for a party.

21

I am a Pisces. That's why I love the water.

I remember sitting in the garden in my mermaid outfit, pissed as a fart watching my fire like it was normal.

When my neighbours were used to me, they knew I was harmless enough just off my nut. So at least I never got put into a mental hospital, asylum, or even a human-sized fish tank.

I probably needed it though I was a danger to myself. Some days I just think, how the fuck did I survive the situations I got myself into.

I was trying to make a point about regressing back to a child with that little tale.

As I said before when you heavy drink or become an alcoholic drinker, your mind kind of stays at that age.

So, I was a 30-year-old woman with a child's mind.

We had a fire in my childhood home. I used to lie in front of it like a cat, and it made me feel safe.

Hence the fires in the garden (which was not safe because I was doing them pissed), but subconsciously I must have been trying to self-soothe even in my pissed-up state.

When we are children, we all love to dress up and make-believe to escape.

I would whack a bloody mermaid outfit on, except I wasn't a child. I was a 30-year-old woman with a daughter, a home, and a job, but at that moment, I was just trying to escape.

Hindsight is beautiful, allowing me to empathise with that version of me now, the version I once hated so very, very much.

I wish I could step back in time and hug that broken girl and tell her this was my path all along, and like the phoenix from the fire, I would rise again after everything around me turned to ash.

One day if you are reading this while in active addiction, I hope you can find some empathy for yourself, some forgiveness, some kindness, and some strength.

If you do not recognise your reflection, one day you will again, and the light will flicker back in your eyes where once they were just pissed blue holes in the snow.

Your skin will not look so transparent, and your breath may not smell like handwash. Whatever divvy made up the myth you cannot smell vodka is an utter bullshitter.

I honestly believed that as well. I only need to smell old dear Deidre's anti-bac gel to take me back to searching my bins for dregs left in the red Glens cap.

I'll never forget that unsatiable craving and how I would be searching the bins hoping there was at least a shot left. It almost brings me to tears thinking about it, that utter desperation. That lack of self-worth. I think of all the times, I sat on buses next to my beautiful darling daughter with a pop bottle half vodka half pop, thinking no one could smell it.

Or all the picnics I would take her on with a bottle in my bag. Remembering all the times I'd get excited over paydays and how I would feel a couple of days later with nothing to my name but regret. When I think of all the happiness, I stole from myself it breaks my heart. All the prominent occasions in life and my daughters' milestones that are blurs. Her bouncing castle birthdays that turned into adult piss ups.

That broken version of me just trying to keep my head above water while being responsible for a little child, a child that I undoubtably adored, and she adored me, yet she deserved so much more. But when you're in denial you even have a problem how can you see these things?

They are normality everyone else is doing it her basic needs are being met she is loved you are doing all you have ever known.

This is how people are supposed to act in relationships rows and ups and downs and everyone drinks it's normal, you go to work so you can't be that bad. People are over reacting it's normal to feel this low isn't it this is just how the world is.

Anyhow here is A poem I wrote called Lost eyes. I wrote this the first time I went into Rehab.

Lost Eyes

I do not Comprehend or recognise
These red, emotionless sad, lost eyes
I do not understand
These scars and bruises on my hands
This body surely cannot be mine
Oh, how it has changed so much and withered in time
What are These words that I'm slurring now?
This can't be me, no way, no how
Where is the girl with the false nails?
The tan seems to of faded to a new shade of pale
Hair is greasy, not washed for days
So far, from those glamorous ways
Spiders upon eyes and cake on the face
Washed away with each mistake
The mirror is dirty upon the wall
The clothes are scattered in the hall
Where is the girl with the world in her grasp?
Is she still living in the deep dark past?
The clothes seemed to of changed
As the mind and the soul got more deranged
This cannot be my reflection
Oozing of pain and neglection
Surely this can't be
Me…
For I do not recognise
These red, emotionless, sad, lost eyes

I Go for Coffee All on My Own

I go for coffee in little cafes all on my own
With my coffee and my thoughts, I do not feel alone
I feel less lonely on my own than I ever have before
I crave for the company of others no longer no more
Not that I do not like other humans, because I do
Bar The odd few
It's just that I sit here dreaming and planning and creating
Not hoping for change, dreading, or shaking
Every day I try to do one positive thing for my mind
Even if it's just choosing to be kind
Instead of putting myself down
So, I sit, and I think about how I've turned life around
I would never have sat in coffee shops alone and content
Now coffee and, dare I say it, cake feel heaven sent
Now though, I just swim a little longer and walk a little faster
It was a coffee and cake, not a cracked-open bottle disaster
I can look in the mirror and acknowledge a fighter with spirit
My cups are half full. There is just something different in it
I go to coffee shops, humble daydreaming on my own
I sit here with a thousand dreams, just me, but not alone

Chapter Three

Procrastination

I wrote this book out into a book handwritten notepad last year. We are now halfway through this year. When I finished it, I was so proud of myself.

A) For completing something because I can start one hundred different tasks and not meet any of them sometimes.
B) For being so raw and honest without entirely hiding behind my poetry the whole time.

I had big plans to publish it, but life got in the way, or so I'd say, as an excuse, and now I'm finally just typing it up.

Note (it's now actually exactly a year since I wrote it in the book, and I am going back and forth changing and adding bits)

I know the reasons why I have put it off.

We can go into that a bit more later. At the time, I had Covid, so I am talking about that a bit. It is currently June (December a year on, erm Feb 2023, one day before my thirty-fifth Birthday, the final deadline I set).

I came back to it again, so I am guessing I proved my point when I wrote about procrastination without ironically taking eight months to fucking type up the book...

Cough, cough, 12 months now. Oh, I can't deal with calculating months. It's been much longer than I thought it would be.

This book has popped into my head every day since it was written there in my little scrapbook, like a little voice from the corner saying, 'TYPE ME,' but I have ignored it, but today I have not, so let us focus on that.

So anyhow, we will go back to where I was writing the book into my little note pad, and at that point, I had covid, you know, that thing that put the world to a standstill and all that divided the maskers and anti-maskers and other similar things I had that.

So, we will go from that point in November sometime.

I am feeling a bit better today, but covid has reminded me of first going into recovery. You start to feel better then suddenly, you wake up with a newfound problem you thought had left ages ago.

When I was first told to isolate, I had many plans to sort out my admin, emails, and many things I have wanted to do for a while.

This has not happened, so for that reason, I can be hard on myself, really, this should have been a time to rest and get better, but my mind just kept creating new jobs for me.

I decided to take care of this by setting myself challenges of one positive thing to do each day.

The principles of marginal gains.

Instead of inundating myself with tick lists, I would do one challenge each day to keep myself focused, then I would reward myself with rest afterward.

This made it easier for me to rest without such a busy mind, that washing machine head stuck on the sin/spin cycle, just not wanting to drain.

I have anxiety and depression anyway, but one of the symptoms of covid is heightened anxiety, and I just was not feeling feeding into that.

So, I cleaned daily so my mind would stay neat.

I sorted through the cupboards and chucked away everything I did not need. I did the niggly jobs around the place that had been pissing me off for ages, but I never got around to doing it. I drank lemsip with honey, ginger, and lemon. I put enough Vicks on my chest to melt through the Antarctic.

I still need to do the admin, though...

I am the person who, if I have a deadline, leaves it till the last minute. I do, do whatever task is at hand, but I put it off until I have no choice but to do it.

I am also all or nothing.

If I am not in the frame of mind to do, it is pointless, So I have listened to my body a bit while I have been poorly.

I can also be the queen of self-sabotage.

So, it could be a little bit of that.

That is why I have left it so long to type up the book. This could be something good and positive, but then I will tell myself it's not. I'm going to look like a twat, but what if it is successful? and it helps people back and forth back and forth until I am like

Oh, fuck off. I'll type it up tomorrow...

Eight months later...

Cough, cough twelve...

Cough, cough, fifteen…

Yeah, whatever, you get the drift.

But now I am ready to do it wholeheartedly, type it and add to it.

When it is finished, publish it, and throw it out to the wind.

So why did I not do that before?

By the way, I am not telling you to take eight months on every decision you make. I am guessing there are a few other overthinking recovering addict minds out there, that do the same things, and I thought if I was open and honest about it, you would be less harsh on yourself.

When you are in recovery, you start to figure out who you are, what makes you tick, what triggers you, what excites you, how to deal with emotions, etc.

I miss my Nan. She was also like a mother figure to me, and I loved her so much. Her hair felt like fluffy clouds, and she could heal anything with a hug.

My Nan died shortly after my Belle was born. I know she is with me. She gives me constant signs. I do not feel so lost now; I truly know that in my heart. She guides me and turns up in my dreams every now and again.

I hope she will be proud of me. She would have stopped people in the street to tell them I had published a book.

She would have adored Belle and my brother's little boy Carter. He is adorable. I love him so much.

One of the greatest gifts of recovery for me is that recently my brother Charlie has asked me to be Carters god mother. It would never in a million years of been an option if I was still drinking. I make time to make sure I keep in touch with Carter, I think I feel so close to him because we share the same Birthday too. My Brother is a wonderful Dad and Carter is funny just like him.

My Nan would have walked over hot coals or broken glass if we were in danger. She was the centre of the whole family, but to me, she felt like the centre of the universe.

When she died, it felt like someone had turned the lights off for a while. I also suspect it was a spark plug igniting some of the wires in my addictive brain.

I felt so lost, but now I can think how lucky I was to know love like that. To give my daughter the warmth in my heart because of what she gave me, and she hasn't left. She has just gone for a while until we meet again.

Here are a couple of poems about my Nan her name was Winnie, but I called her Nanny Win.

Nanny Win

How did you always get your roasters fluffy but crispy?
I tried all kinds of methods, Nan; I hope you're not lonely, and
you don't miss me
Well, of course, I miss you, but I will see you when the time is
right
No one ever made a ham sandwich like you; it was like you
sprinkled on fairy light
Sometimes I put a whole bottle of comfort in the washing
machine
You still visit me in my dreams
I do it to make it smell like yours,
You were always doing house chores
I do not wake up sad like I used too anymore
Maybe that's why I like sleeping so much, hoping to see your
face once more
You felt like home, and your skin was so soft
I loved your hair like candy floss
Birthdays and Christmases pass by, and I wish
I could hold your hands and feel your forehead kiss
I will, though I know, and I can't grieve forever, or I will not
live
I know now that sober, I have got so much more to give
I hope it didn't make you sad as you saw me stumble
I can almost taste your apple crumble
I feel all funny still after all these years when I pass your home
Still know off by heart your house phone
I am going to be honest; I was a little lost when you left for a
while
I am ok now though I've found my smile
I know that you were old and, in the end, in pain
You used to hate it when people said your whole name
To us, though, you were Nanny Win, our very own queen
Next time you visit, please bring me roasters in my dream

Spirit Guide

The steps that we walk will be different from those of our
predecessors
We may hear whispers in the winds from our ancestors
What say 'go this way that way
And you say, 'which way, what way?'
But on each path, we take, we drop little pebbles, little marks
upon stone
Even when we walk towards a place unknown
That path was already created with our name upon it
With songs sung in our name that flow like a sonnet
For one day, we will be another's ancestor, and they will talk of
their family tree
There will be songs in our names that are sung with glee
For we will be
The producers of memories
So, let's not leave the lines empty
Fill them with words a plenty
So that when people take footsteps, they get a Deja view
Because they see flashbacks of our trod paths that were walked
by you
What is the meaning of it all? Do our dreams give us clues like
a riddle?
Are we in between worlds, somewhere in the middle?
Who knows
They know
Our ancestors and forefathers built old stone houses painted
black and white.
The ones that whisper this way, that way, late at night
Listen to them; they are guiding you softly. They can't do the
work
They are the little orbs of light that heal your hurt
We accept history, and we predict future times
Yet we follow strict paths and walk in straight lines
Take a detour
Want more
Fight through the routines
Dance within the moonbeams

Remember...
There were people before us, and there will be people long after
we are gone.
So, make deep steps in the stone to guide the future, so our
memory lives on.

I couldn't think about my nan before it hurt too much I used to think. Fuck emotions!

Yes, we must sit with them now, not just push them down with whiskey, yak I hate emotions, but the more you sit in them, the less they start hurting not saying I'm the stone woman and you should start calling me medusa, but I don't crumble at the thought of them now.

Do you know what little thing made emotions feel ten times worse?

Our addiction override.

They intensified feelings tenfold, so we thought we could not handle them and needed substance to survive them.

Our addiction made us dependent on it, but claiming back your power and building yourself up bit by bit is pretty badass. We are not vulnerable little children, and that's how our addiction made us feel.

Like finding out Santa wasn't real for the first time.

That first crush you had rejecting you.

Your parents divorcing.

Losing your first grandparent.

The Lion King. (You know the scene)

That e17 song.

When Britney shaved her head.

When Friends ended (not just on a break)

When I realised, I could never actually be a blue avatar.

Free willy jumping over the fire.

The little princess cries out for poppa.   (Oh, that got me)

When my dad would not buy me those millennium rock ports.

Gladiator when he puts his hands through the corn fields.

Green Mile.

Pearl Harbour.

Still pissed off that Rose did not make room for Jack on that door. (Bitch)

Oh god, that was hard.

The list is endless. You also, and this is a shocker, realise the person you thought you were in active addiction to is nothing like who you are now, in fact, the opposite.

Now you crave peace, anything good for you emotionally, physically, and mentally.

I thought about going into a dictionary and putting lodes of big words in this book to make me sound clever.

That's not me; I intend to reach a different audience. (I have used Grammarly and been at war over the English/American versions of words though. They just want to put a Z in everything)

This does not mean we are not intelligent, streetwise, or have a wealth of life skills and knowledge. It means our vocabulary may not be one of the extraordinary words we cannot spell.

I swear a lot, it is naughty, but it is relatable. If I want you to see I am a human too, then hiding behind a dictionary using words I would not usually use would be deceiving and a toxic trait of trying to be something I am not.

Unfortunately, no matter what you do, someone will read it and think what a load of drivel, common woman words, etc. Someone may relate to it, though, because they can understand it.

If I made my readers feel stupid by using words, I did not understand in the first place to look good, then that would defeat the object of what I am trying to do. So, after that internal battle, I decided not to let my own fear drag other people down in the process and to own who I actually am.

I avoid anything that looks toxic now.

I have, however, had lots of mini-mental relapses. Although I have not picked up a bottle and drunk alcohol, I have done things gone out of my way to do something that I knew would harm my well-being. Afterward, I processed and analysed it and tried understanding the route course.

Fundamentally the word that comes up for me the most is FEAR.

When you are in a state of fear, you are low down on the well-being chart.

The lowest is the feeling of shame.

This is a feeling that I was engulfed in when I first entered recovery.

The highest being enlightenment followed by peace.

It can sometimes go back to simple things like Maslow's hierarchy of needs.

Since being in recovery, I have feelings of enlightenment and inner peace, which is truly blissful.

So where does this feeling of fear come from?

The fear of losing this feeling of peace and enlightenment? I have never felt before.

The fear of living a life with the truly authentic version of myself. If people do not like this version, they will not like me. No masks to hide behind?

The fear of succeeding?

(What will I moan about then?)

The fear of failing?)

(I can hear 'I told you so' before I have even done anything, who do you think you are?)

The fear of letting go of this victim mindset mentality.?

The fear of cutting the ties of the past, for then I will be free. What can I blame bad decisions on?

The fear of being a laughingstock, someone who flew far above her station, come back down to the floor where you belong, and you come to hide under this rock. You are a caterpillar, not a butterfly.

You are a Butterfly

I have always loved the process of a butterfly
I am sure when it's a caterpillar heavy and sluggish, it does not
know it will one day fly.
In the complete process of it, no one looks at a caterpillar and
saw beauty
Yet when it emerges a butterfly, the beauty is there for all to see
It is still the same insect that was hatched into a crawling
creature
Yet it cocoons itself and grows a beautiful new feature
That gives it the ability to not only look pleasant but fly
I am sure when it was just a caterpillar, it did not know it could
reach trees so high
The once birds who looked upon it like prey
It can fly with now, although they say a butterfly's life can last
only a day
If that is true, imagine everything it would see that day with a
different view.
You may see a caterpillar, but I can see the butterfly in you
So, if you ever feel cocooned in darkness, know one day, you
will emerge
A new person who can now keep up with the birds
Who you spent your whole previous life fearing?
That is why I find the butterfly so endearing
Addiction, mental illness, grief, and pain
It can make you feel like a caterpillar caught out in the rain
But now, there is a process, and you will not always be
A caterpillar looking up at a butterfly in a tree
For one day, after you grieve or lose your own toxic life cycle,
you grow
Into a butterfly that spreads its newfound wings like a beautiful
show

As you can see, the list is endless; however, once you know what the issue is, you can sift through it.

Work through it piece by piece using a tool called my irrational belief process.

People in recovery tend to have low self-esteem initially and are consumed by self-doubt. They have lost this imaginary shield of confidence that came in the form of alcohol, drugs, or five-minute highs. They are laid bare to the world for the first time in their adult lives.

Where does she pull this information?

I get this information from the meetings or groups I have been to.

Not that I am sitting there like a weird little mole with a recording device.

I feel people's pain from the conversations I have had. That sounds like I attend these meetings to get data and information.

I do not. I just listen to the pain in people's voices. I relate to how they talk about themselves with such low disregard and hold themselves back through fear of the unknown, which makes me feel less alone.

I can now appear confident and assertive in social situations, but my mind attacks me from all angles when I am alone.

I am drafting this book in the hope that I can make other people feel less alone.

I shared at a meeting once about how I get a wave of depression after I do something positive.

How it's like self-sabotage or a comedown of sorts after a high.

I am always chasing the next high, the next project, the following poem, and I never ever give myself time to appreciate, reflect and be proud.

That's because those feelings are foreign to me, and I get imposter syndrome and think I need to get a grip. I am just doing what ordinary people do.

I don't like compliments. They make me feel so awkward. I feel like I could just crawl inside my own skin.

I usually hit back with an insult about myself to even it out, for example.

'I like your outfit. You look nice today.'

'Oh, thanks. It's from a charity shop. I thought I'd brush my hair today because the rest of the week I've looked like shit.'

I don't know why I do that.

Well, I kind of do, I loved Eminem as a kid, and in his movie Eight Mile, he is in this rap battle. He says all the insults he thinks his opponent will say about him, so his opponent has nothing to say in return.

This method has been my great defence and works wonders in an argument. However, it's flowed through to everything.

I put myself down so others cannot do it first, but why do that when someone compliments you?

So, I am trying to learn to accept them gracefully with a 'thank you, so do you or 'that's so kind of you to say'

It's more complicated than you think, lowering these defences and becoming a more vulnerable version of yourself in those moments. That's when fear creeps in.

Recovery is re-learning everything. Every toxic trait you picked up along the way, the ones you do automatically because they are ingrained in you.

I realised in active addiction, there was comfort in pain. I knew that feeling inside out. It was familiar. It was guilt, fear, shame, and resentment, and it wrapped around me like a miserable comfort blanking, keeping me isolated from the world.

You do terrible things to yourself because you know the outcome will be you being wrapped in that comfort zone of the shit city you are used to.

So why fear success?

Why not want it with every inch of your being in recovery?

You have made the first step. The world is your oyster, indeed?

It's because these are unknown feelings.

The unknown is scary, and even more so, every positive step you take forward toward your future is a further step away from your past.

Your past was your identity, fucking shit up was part and parcel, and well, it wasn't really your fault you have/had an addiction.

Moving forward and taking control of your life and accountability for failures, successes, and all the in-betweens feels like a lot of pressure.

It makes you want to lie in your bed and take an exceptionally long nap, maybe even suck your thumb, and think, am I capable of these things? Can I really be a success?

So, we procrastinate through fear and worry until we are at a crossroads, and we have no choice but to choose one way or another.

We haven't the choice of being indecisive here. A bit like deadlines. Why do we do it the day before the deadline? get all in a panic and stressed etc, because it causes adrenalin. It's like a buzz. Will I make it on time?

It's a chance for us to fail. While we try to push through, how many times have we said diet starts Monday and Monday never comes, then it's a week before you must fit into that dress you brought two sizes too small, and you are like, for fuck's sake, so you eat cabbage juice for a week instead.

I started to ask myself what the point was in doing successful things if it was just going to give me a wave of depression after?

If I did not benefit emotionally from it, until I remembered I am an addict. Although not drinking actively, I still have an addict's brain.

So, if my addiction cannot get to me through guilt, fear, and shame to refuel my desire to drink, it will go for my dreams, ambitions, and desires instead.

This revolution, to me, was a bit shitty. I was like 'fuck you, brain, you dickhead'

During my recovery, I have also tried to educate myself on this mysterious disease that wants me dead.

Armour up and know your enemy.

One of the courses I took explained how at one point, alcohol protected me from feelings of danger or things too painful I could not cope with on my own.

Our brains are hardwired fundamentally to protect us from danger. So however, warped it may seem in some fucked up, weird kind of way, it's trying to protect you. It conveniently forgets the absolute joke of a shit storm that comes after the two-second feelings of protection.

It all sounds complicated, but it's not when broken into bite-sized pieces.

Write down your fears, and possible solutions.

An Example. I fear relapse, I will actively show up for myself on the days I don't feel I need support are the days I need it the most.

If you are a bit dramatic like me, you can burn them. It is so freeing to burn your fears, like bye bitch burn...

Write down a list of things you forgive yourself for and what you will do to amend those things if it is safe and ok to do so.

An Example I forgive myself for some of the people I hurt in the process, I will try to be more considerate of other people's feelings as well as my own.

(This can be so healing to your inner child.)

Write down your hopes, dreams, and desires.

(Example) I am going to publish this book. It will help other people, it will help me to heal.

You could even do a creative vision board for it.

This way, you actively put it out to the universe like the law of attraction.

Here are a few poems I have written on the matter.

The Law of Attraction

First, write it down for it to be received
Once words hit paper, it can be believed
Focus on it every day
Believe in your own words that you say
A negative mindset can attract adverse action
Like having a minus number and then hitting it with subtraction
For example, 'oh, it's raining, that's just my luck'
Mother nature's not just out to get you. She gives not one fuck
If you have spent two hours straightening your hair
She didn't go, 'yes that house is hers. I'm going to rain right there.'
If you wake up with the mindset you are going to be late
You have already got yourself worked up in a state
So, each traffic light seems to stay on red
Till it's boiling, piss right out of your head
Change the mindset and calm the storm
Wake up 10 minutes earlier and appreciate the dawn
Ground yourself with the day read the forecast
Let those anxious feelings just Wizz right past
Don't store them up and let them bubble
For they will only lead you to trouble
Take one good thing out of each day
If it's a bad one, better ones are on the way
There is nothing terrible about lessons learned
Practice what you preach, for dreams are earned
If you are feeling low or depressed
Practice, if you can, some mindfulness
Breathe all the way in slowly breathe out
Don't harbour that fear and doubt...

I forgive myself.

I release from my mind all the days I destroyed
Trying to fill the unfillable void
The never-ending insatiable itch
That left me bleeding in a ditch
I forgive myself for not sooner finding another way
For I could only break free after my darkest day
For all the days, I hated myself and hung my head in shame
Il fight for who you are and rebuild your name
I will fight daily with all my strength to quiet this disease
That sucks from your soul like ravines fleas
For all those still suffering il keep you in my mind
I wish to myself then I had been a little kind
How can you be kind though to a reflection you don't know?
You still reap the repercussions of those seeds you did sow
Your still there somewhere under the wreck and the rubble
The path that you are walking will only lead you to trouble
I have appeared from the darkness with a flashlight in hand
So, if you need a friend, then I understand
Times now more than ever, seem like a messed-up movie
Now I choose to live life without substance to soothe me
Well, it only comforted me for a second or so
Then the walls all came down on the never-ending shit show
If every day, I aspire to get just one percent better
Not aiming for unreachable stars or to be a jet setter
Just a humble life trying to help some of you
Because, believe me, I know what you have been through
I look back at my reflection and see the light back in my eyes
To the days of destruction, I bid you fair well and say my
goodbyes...

Testing, Testing 123

I had a mocktail the other day, even the placebo of it filled me with guilt
I'm trying to get out in the world but just want to hide home under my quilt
I want to be able to do the things ordinary people can do without anxiety
I can't, though, and after a while, I must slip out quietly
When I drank, I was bold and brash, and loud?
I did things that didn't make me feel proud
I drank, though, to self-medicate
Now without that safety net, I get all in a state
I went to a party earlier and saw my friends I love so much
But I felt nervous and anxious and out of touch
Because there was no drink to hide behind in my hand
My emotions took over something I had never planned
I cried in the taxi I thought by now, I should stop finding it such an ordeal, quite a lot
But seeing drink everywhere is like taking a diabetic child into a candy shop
And saying look at what you cannot have because it's bad for you
Oh, look at that boy sucking sour lollipops. It turned his tongue blue
You can't keep hiding from everything, for the people you care for, you want to show up
But then your addiction overrides your mind and tries to interrupt
Look at them having fun, bet you wish you could go on., Just have a sip it will make your chest feel warm
Then you feel your mind battling as your emotions get torn
So, you say your goodbyes
Don't want the people you love to see you cry
Then you think, why can't I just be normal and not be a nervous, anxious freak
Why couldn't I activate pilot mode like I do so in the week
They are going to think I'm rude or that I am making it all about me

I should be over it by now, think it's an excuse and doubt me
Deep down, though, I know my friends are reasonable people,
and they support me
One thing this recovery business has taught me
Is it trying to find chinks in your armour so it can strike?
Generally, in the depths of the night
In black and white, it's just someone who can't drink alcohol,
easy solution then do not drink
But it is far more than that, it's a daily attack, a daily battle that
tries to override what you think
Some days you can quieten it quickly, others it seems to
scream, wanting that feed
Your eardrums vibrate so loud with it, it feels as though they
could bleed
On the surface, though you smile, you help others, you present
well
Because you don't want people seeing this internal hell
I know I cannot have it. It's not up for debate
I Can replay the scenario and fast forward to the tape
But today, though, even though this turmoil, this pain, this
choice
I chose not to listen to my addictions voice

Wolvo Girl

I was just sitting in the window watching passers-by
Then a heart-breaking sight caught my eye
A young girl in her twenties, I'd say
With infected scabs on her face and hair like hay
With frail legs underneath her skirt
And fingernails covered in dirt
Her eyes are like spaceships
Clothes hanging from her hips
She comes up to the bins and gets out the fags
To collect them up to get fresh drags
I'm presuming in a home-rolled burn
She rotates around Wolverhampton, trying to earn
Begging, stealing, shoplifting coffee
Teeth are like they are covered in toffee
She's not even thirty
Living this life must make her feel dirty
Then again, I doubt she feels anything but the need for another
fix
When things are tight, throws 8% larger in the mix
Just to help to keep her numb
It is daytime now at night-time is when the married men have
their fun
But they label her the crooked one
She's just feeding her addiction
While men use her like a blow-up doll to indulge in fantasies
and fiction
You know, the prostitutes like in les mis west end shows
Ran out of veins, injects her toes
What kind of life is this
Leaning up post shouting any business
While men in blacked-out cars drive through
Lie back, close your eyes, and pretend it is not happening,
nothing new.
Money for the pot
The spoon will soon be boiling hot
But behind every woman turned to skin and bone
Was once a frightened child all alone

Until one day, they numbed the pain with a substance in their
vein
How desperate must you have to be more desperate than a
frosty jack lover counting pennies?
Or a coke whore riding old men
Stimulating adrenaline with amphetamine
Prescription morphine by the bottle bright green
That you slipped from your Nan as a teen
A million other forms, no one better than the other,
Still, someone's daughter with a heartbroken father, lost child,
and hurting Mother.

One thing it's made me realise now is I fear no one. No one can
do anything worse to me than what my own mind tries to do at
night, than the internal battle I have going on inside my head.

Some days it is quieter than others, but some days it screams
so loud it could make my eardrums bleed, and that, my friend,
makes you powerful because each day you do not give in is
another day won.

Chapter Four

Triggers and How to Deal with Them

So, as I am writing this, it is November. Well, it was November when I hand-wrote the book. Remember what I told you about before I made my point with the procrastination part, irony ay.

So, we are entering the season to be jolly soon, which means every other advertisement on the television will be full of festive families drinking and glorifying the process of drinking. Most people get pissed from Christmas to the new year, and the shops extend the alcohol aisle to the whole shop.

I remember when I first went into recovery, I went into ASDA, and I needed to get some dog food, and opposite the dog food was rows and rows of alcohol, making me want to cry. My method back then was out of sight, out of mind.

So, the Christmas period does make it a little bit harder. However, I have had a couple of sober Christmases, and they weren't as painfully awful as I'd imagined them to be. I woke up fresh and saw the true beauty in my daughter's face when she opened her presents.

I got to be part of helping her make beautiful childhood memories instead of the entire day being revolved around how much alcohol I could guzzle and not really remembering all that much.

The good thing about typing this up now is that I know what happened at Christmas. It was a lovely day. My brother Henry stayed on the night, and a guy I had been seeing for a while (we have been together two years at this point, you will hear about him later) came around on Christmas eve.

We played UNO and a few other games. It was adorable. I waited nine months to introduce this person to my daughter and didn't rush. In fact, it was the first sober relationship I've had. My daughter's father never called her on Christmas day, and she had tried him several times, but his phone was off.

Things like this used to really trigger me. She is my world, and I could not understand how he would not want to talk to her on the phone. There was so much resentment there it used to make me ill.

However, I try not to let it bother me as it once did. Handing my power over to him and letting him see he still can affect my emotions is not something I give away as freely now. Of course, I hate seeing my daughter upset.

The difference is now I am sober, I am present. It's not a justified excuse for me to get smashed because when you think about it from my daughter's point of view, that was a double whammy, Daddy is not there, and Mommy is intoxicated over it. Who has she got to rely on, then?

The best way to deal with these things now is to block him. My daughter has a phone. If he wants to speak to her, he can contact on there. I will not make that choice for my daughter for him to twist around and make her resent me and hate me in the future.

However, it's been over ten years of back and forth, and it takes up too much of my energy trying to get a level of consistency from him that he is incapable of giving.

I empathise with him somewhat because I know what it is like to be locked in that cycle. Still, I must protect my own sanity because I am the primary carer for my daughter, so my recovery must come first for her sake, so anything that affects her negatively I must remove may seem harsh, but it's true.

So, like I said, it is August/Jan, you get the drift, as I am typing this, which may just seem like one big contradiction on the procrastination chapter, but there is no point in me typing this out if I cannot be truthful and admit to my own downfalls. I was talking about the Christmas period, but I find summer much harder.

It is far more socially acceptable in the summer months for people to day drink, the sun is out BBQ on and drinks in hand. A couple of weeks ago, I faced one of the worst challenges so far: attending my best friends' daughters' eighteenth birthday party.

I love this girl very much and have been there since she was a baby, and I did not have it in my heart not to go.

It was painful, emotionally, seeing this baby I had watched grow as an eighteen-year-old being able to drink while someone she looked up to couldn't.

I know she was proud of me for getting sober, and she wouldn't look at it like that, but they were the kind of tricks my head played on me that day.

My childhood friends were all there drinking, the ones I had done all my drinking with, and I just felt so lonely it that moment. I didn't think years on it would affect me the way it did, but I left after a while and burst out crying. I hardly ever cry anymore.

(Amelia, I am so proud of you, and it has been beautiful watching the process of you turn from a baby into a woman. You were my first little love, and you will always be my baby making dinosaur kingdoms and putting glitter everywhere. I love you princess.)

However, I had my daughter with me. It was a one-off occasion and a learning curve. I am not ready for things like that just yet, it was one of my biggest challenges, and I never drank even though parts of me so desperately wanted to. My recovery side, which wants good for me, put up a fight like it had never put up before. I hugged my daughter. We ordered food, So I emotionally ate instead, but it was still better than a bottle of vodka, and it was another day won. Although very painful, it made me stronger and another big step away from the person I used to be.

Back to November, we put decorations up on the tree without it falling on top of me at some point. I remember consuming so much whiskey one year I sweated it out, and it burned my skin.

My life is obviously a lot quieter now. I don't go to as many parties or pubs around this season. However, looking back at the end of my addiction, I isolated myself anyway. I wouldn't contemplate attending a party unless I drank half a bottle of vodka while getting ready.

I do not have to wake up now thinking fuck, who did I insult last night? In those horrors where you remember nothing until your friends fill you in on your antics. Or when they stop partying, you go home alone and stop at a garage on the way to drink at home alone until you pass out.

Waking up in the morning with a craving that consumes your whole body, until you're at the off license at seven a.m. begging to be served, even though you know they cannot help you then.

The bills pile up in your draws as you move your finances around to feed your addiction. You look at the electric meter, wondering how long three pounds will last.

You have spent all your money, so you must pluck up the courage to make calls to borrow some, or you go around the house collecting change just enough to get that cheap version of Lambrini that rips your tummy apart and tastes as sour as apple cider vinegar.

I use a tool called playthings forward (like that mike skinner tune).

You have a thought pop in your head like, 'Oh, I would love a drink right now.'

I fast forward from the taste of the first drink to the worst-case scenario. I picture my daughter's little face with tears rolling down it. I imagine the disappointment in everyone who now feels so proud of me.

Whenever I get the urge to drink, I think of rattling in a hospital bed, seeing the lights, and hearing the voices of the nurses that must think what a waste of a life.

I take myself back to a room full of social services, police, teachers, and my keyworker, and I remember that utter feeling of shame, fear, and regret as they discuss the person, I love more than anything.

My actual heartbeat and discuss how my actions have endangered her.

They ripped me to shreds, they bare-faced lied, and I did not know what I was going into. I was like a rabbit in the headlights.

When this newly qualified social worker approached mine, my dog's lead was on the floor. In the social report, he labelled it as a noose.

Now that changes the definition of dog lead, doesn't it? It makes it sound like a hazardous object and not, in fact, a dog lead.

My daughter was eight at the time. There was a lighter in the bathroom. He labelled it as a dangerous object, ok should there have been a lighter in the bathroom? In an ideal world, no, but how many people have lighters in their bathrooms without them being labelled as a firearm.

He put how none of my drawers in the kitchen had locks on so she could grab knives.

If you come to my house now, three years on sober different life different world, you would see my daughter's room is immaculate. She has always kept it that way with her dollies all in certain places. She has lined them up in specific rows since she was about two years old.

In his report, though, he put that Isabella keeps her room neat and tidy to escape the chaos of the rest of her world.

Literally just pulled it out of thin air and came to that conclusion.

I could write more, but it's winding me up, so I am not going to because it makes me angry for all the other people who need support, not a public assassination.

If I wasn't a wreck, they wouldn't have had access to me to make those assumptions, so it's not a woo-is-me moment. More of a message to those in this situation so you can see how things can be twisted.

Also, know your rights to get representation or citizen's advice and request all social work documentation before the meeting. Look at the safeguarding law about core meetings and documentation.

I only know this now because of the job I do. I have had to do safeguarding courses because I am now, ironically, a safeguarding lead.

No one can hate the addict more than the addict hates themself.

Of course, something needed to happen, but it just made me feel worse. It made me want to kill myself ten times more if I am honest.

A part of me thinks, is that what those meetings intend to do, break someone's spirit so bad it makes or breaks them?

As a mother, you would die for your child. You would turn into a mother bear and fight the universe for your child, so to be sitting in a room with strangers discussing whether you cause harm to your child is beyond explainable.

It is heart-wrenching. Are they talking about somebody else? It can't be you, not your baby. How could they be talking about you?

How have you gotten to this point?

How can you get yourself out of this hole you have dug into and dragged an innocent beautiful child into too?

Will she grow up to think this is normal?

Will she grow up to be an alcoholic and feel this unbearable pain that eats her up from the inside out?

Now the weight of that thought is too much to handle, but statistics say children become a product of their environment.

So, is not drinking wine with my Christmas dinner hard? No, not really, when you think about where that wine can take you.

When you drink alcohol, you are vulnerable. You are almost like a child yourself. Your life is up for discussion.

I love being in control of my feelings, words, and emotions now.

I love that I can provide my daughter with a stable home full of love and laughter. I was always very honest with my daughter.

She knew I went to rehab to get well.

She saw things she should not have seen when I was drinking. Fights and arguments, uncontrollable tears, a house that was a mess when the housework just got too much, irrational behaviour, snappy mommy in the morning, fun mommy with a drink, then sad mommy.

My bad choices were terrible, but she got dragged into them too.

I will spend my every waking breath protecting her from ever having to see me so unwell again. This has taught my daughter that adults make mistakes, but if you have accountability for your actions and learn from your mistakes, you can achieve wonderful things.

This year my daughter has a good role in the school play. She's beyond overjoyed. I was never a mother who missed plays.

I was always extra on the Easter bonnet parade. I took her and her friend's places, I did parties for her, and her room was filled with toys, but everything I did every single thing I did, I did it with a bottle in my bag, rather than focusing on the joy of my daughter's face.

I was thinking about my next drink. When I was drinking, my daughter was a closed book. She wouldn't even tell me what she had for lunch at school some days. You can only understand why once you are out of that situation looking in.

I do now.

What money will she get today?

Will she kick off if I tell her I'm being bullied?

Will she cry?

Shall I just say nothing at all?

That thought breaks my heart, but I cannot change the past; however, I can try every day to be the best version of myself for Isabella and its crazy to say this, but for myself to because I deserve to be happy.

The gift of recovery has helped me find joy in every moment, treasure every memory and be stable enough to give advice.

My daughter tells me about her day at school, her playground problems, hopes, fears, and everything in between.

We do affirmations on the night. It's just such a good feeling of contentment when my daughter, dog, and I cuddle up and talk about our days. We also have a board, which helps us keep to a routine.

Each thing gets ticked off, like getting ready for school, helping, etc. She must get five ticks a day. Then on a Friday, she gets her pocket money.

Before, I was just giving it to her. In fairness, I have been guilty of showering her with gifts, but I realised that I was not teaching her the value of money or that things need to be earned. Obviously, she is an only child.

I was one of five, so I did not want her to get that lone child spoilt brat mentality either.

This poem I will put here now is so personal because my heart was breaking when I wrote this. As I said before, this person was a massive trigger for me. It was unbearable to watch repeatedly but, unfortunately, out of my control. I wanted it to be Isabella's choice of what she wanted to do about it, and I never wanted to make those choices for her, so she would grow up to resent me.

I have had to change how I react to it now because it bubbled me up inside with so much rage it made me feel physically ill.

I would scream and shout and want to cause all the havoc and chaos in the world to get the point across.

However, it's been over two years since I wrote this poem. Things have not changed, just the way I deal with them. I was fuelling the fire playing straight into the hands of this profile that had been created of me of this pissed-up psychopath.

I guess I was, but I had my reasons; I just should have handled situations better.

I had the same situation happen today, and I have realised now that some people just want to steal your peace. They want to put zero effort in but are bitter and twisted that you have achieved something they cannot.

They wallow in self-pity and narcissism that overrides even the love for a young, innocent girl, if that girl can be used in the crossfire to get the desired reaction they want.

To me, there is nothing sicker and more twisted than that.

I never went out of my way to deliberately hurt anyone. However, I am now able to hold accountability if I do. Face up to any wrongdoings. Some people simply just cannot do that. It is not part of their agender it hinders the perfect image they believe they have painted of themselves.

What's that saying?

Real eyes realise real lies.

I see you now, I see all of the people who thought I was some kind of laughingstock or joke or took my kindness for weakness. I can almost hear them hissing before they come. Snakes can hide in the shadows but at some point, the sun will come out, and their skin will shed.

I imagine you will understand the frustrations when you read this poem.

Window PAIN

She waits by the window
Watches the cars flow
The sun rises the sun did go
Still no sign of daddy though

She does not want fancy things
Just the sound of his voice when the phone rings
But the phone does not ring,
Does he understand the sadness that brings?

Sometimes he calls her daily, and she gets so excited to hear his
voice
Then he disappears for weeks on end, leaving her no choice
But to listen to the answering machine
'Mommy, why does Daddy be so mean?'

He promises her things he has no intention of getting
She falls for it every time, forgetting
The thousand promises he has made before
'Another chance, Mommy, please one more?'

Stuck in the middle, how many times can I watch her cry?
As another Birthday passes by
All I asked him to get last year were banners and balloons
But he turned up late half-cut doing something far more
important, I presume

She does not want pretty presents wrapped in a box
She wants to not have to watch the clock tick and toc
You see, it is passing by this year. She's nine
As she waits by the window wanting to unwrap his time

Belle's Dad or his friends or family if you are reading this, please understand this has not been done to hurt or undermine the love I know that he has for Isabella.

I do not benefit from wanting to see him where I used to be, and I want nothing more than for him to be able to have the same joy that I have in watching her grow.

Maybe this book can be a stark reminder of all she went through and how beautiful her life is now. If you want help into recovery, I will help you with open arms but until that day unfortunately we cannot relive it again, it kind of defeats the object of me getting well if she still gets subjected to that world.

Do people still trigger me?

Fuck yes….

I've learned to act differently to it. We all have a moral inventory of principles and how we believe we should handle the situation or how we should behave. So, it's hard not to take it personally when people disappoint us or don't give us the answers or actions, we think we deserve.

I have realised I cannot control other people's actions or choices but only how I react.

I don't always get it right, but I'm getting better. We are the centre of our own universe, so they are the centre of theirs.

There are other mitigating factors. Have they had a difficult day?

Are they tired, hungry, or depressed?

What is going on in their head?

Not going to try to pick apart those things anymore. I can be the queen of analysing, stressing worrying, so now I tell myself the past is the past I cannot change it. The future I cannot predict it.

All have is the here and now.

There are many words and sayings that stuck with me in recovery, and that one is so true.

How much time do we spend worrying about what he said, she said, we said in the past? How much time do we stress about things that haven't happened yet?

We never let ourselves live in the moment.

Some people might trigger us, and we can remove them because they are toxic and move on, or to the people, we have no choice but for them to be in our life, or we are going to see them at work, family occasions, school, etc. we love them, but they trigger the fuck out of us. In that case, learn how to put boundaries. At first, this can be extremely hard saying no to people we've always said yes to.

When I used to see my key worker, she told me about something called PAC, which stands for parent, adult, and child.

This doesn't just have to be the case with a parent. It can be in any relationship, so say, for example...

You have a friendship, and because of your addiction, you took on the role of the child. They took on the part of the parent. That's how you want to act, stamping your feet, shouting, etc. The healthy way would be to show some assertiveness and respond as an adult. Here are some examples.

Friend, 'do you think you're responsible enough now to do that?'

You 'how dare you blah blah blah.'

How it could go if you respond as an adult is

'Thank you for your worry and concern, and I appreciate my past actions; you may feel that way. However, I have moved on from being that person now. I would appreciate it if you could take me on the merit of who I am now and not who I was.'

When anger is met with anger, it's a case of butting heads, however, when you respond as an adult, it puts you back in the driving seat instead of throwing your dummy out of the pram.

Everywhere you go, in public, there will be a huffy Karen or posh Paul who looks down upon people, but that's on them, not you.

Let them live life their way, fucking complaining, and trying to drag people down to massage their own ego.

Go about your day, another little nugget of a saying.

'It's absolutely none of my business for other people's opinions are of me.'

I used to spend my whole life wanting to be liked, liked by people who now I couldn't give two single fucks about. I hated the thought of people not liking me. It churned me up inside and gave me sleepless nights.

Not everyone will like me, I don't like everyone. However, now I don't hate anyone. I don't care enough to waste time, energy, and effort on that negativity. People say when you go to AA or NA listen out for the similarities rather than the differences.

If you take this kind of philosophy into life, even with people you don't particularly like all that much, you can learn to have a level of empathy.

For example, victim mindset people

'Why do dreadful things always happen to me? That's just my luck.'

Think that person might be having a bit of a shitter or series of past events that have led them to believe that way.

So however, annoying it is, they mean no offense, and it's just something ingrained in them. In life, people will come and go. Some people will leave imprints on your heart and mind; others will not.

During active addiction, there were so many great feuds I had with people I don't give a second thought about now.

I try hard to limit the toxic energy I'll let in my life now. I'm far from perfect there are people I'm sure I have hurt or offended along the way. Sorry sincerely if I owe you an apology if, on the off chance, you are reading this, I apologise. I'm trying to be a better person now.

Don't hand your power over to people who don't deserve it. Some people go to ALDI looking for a row because they're unhappy in their own life. There is power in silence in keeping your peace, or if they really push your buttons, a condescending smile, and the middle finger,) but that's a last resort, don't go getting into scraps by the fruit and veg.)

The worst kind is spiritual vampires. They see the empath's energy a mile off. They see a person doing well and think I want that. I should have that. I'm going to take that. That vibrant energy she or he has, I'm going to suck from it and fill myself up.

The problem is that your positive, kind-hearted energy and nature do not belong in them; they only wanted it because it was yours. So, they take your energy but don't put it to practical use. They just wait till yours has run out and find another source. They can't get what you have because they do not want to put in the demanding work and effort, but at least if they take your energy from you, you won't have it either.

I should know this pattern by heart by now, but these people do not present like that. It takes a few months to realise that, that much stuff cannot happen to one person, so therefore, you have a shelf life too.

That's what hurts the most in the, because what you thought was genuine, in fact, was not at all.

On your behalf, it was, but on theirs, there was always an agender. You will never win with these kinds of people, the reason being when you are filled with empathy for others and continuously try to save the world, they have none at all, and even while they are sitting with a bucket full of your energy, they have drained, they will turn round flip it and say it was all your fault and make you doubt yourself.

This was not my first time at this mistake, though, and part of me wanted to stop helping everyone because I was sick of getting burned, losing myself in the process, and feeling utterly deflated.

However, there are some genuine people I have had the privilege of helping, and why should those people miss out because of the vampires lurking about.

I hate to think of people like that, even when the evidence is there in black and white in front of me, it's like I still want to believe this person or people are good people at the core of them, and it's excruciatingly painful when you realise, they are not.

I've done these dances for years on end with people, but now the moment you show me your colours, and when I've scratched behind all the rainbows and glitter you represented with and all I see is grey, I retract.

I had so much to say on the matter, at times to hurt back the people who had hurt me, or explain things from my perspective, that after exhausting myself with it spinning around my mind, I had nothing left to say at all.

I choose peace when, before, I would have thrived on war. Like your energy turns hollow in them, so will your words, perspective, and pain. It will go nowhere. The other party will not accept it as accurate, so what's the point?

As I said before, violence is in silence.

Not the kind that is passive-aggressive, but choosing peace when they want war.

Choosing silence when they want words, they want to hear that they have hurt you, then when all else fails, they will parade their newfound source on a pedal stall Infront of you, like a shiny new diamond.

Them things used to hurt but now I just think that poor person is on a ticking timer too, some may last longer than others, but ultimately their time will come.

Should I warn them?

What's the point?

They will not listen anyway because they will be at the beginning of the grooming stages where you are getting loved bombed, and you can't believe that anyone else on the planet would try to be mean to this person.

How unfair it is that terrible things always happen to this wonderful person etc. Little do you know you will be put under a series of mini tests to check just how far they can push you, how loyal you are how much they can take. They wouldn't be mean to you in the first place, would they?

You would never give them access to your energy source that way.

Note to self-stop trying to save people, stop giving away my heart so quickly, build that force field around myself, so they may chink the armour but never get in again. Stop touching the fire, then crying when I get burned, dance in the rain, and moan when I get wet. You get the gist.

So, in conclusion, try not to let people trigger you, put in boundaries and use the good old Google to look up parent adult child. That will explain it better than I can. When you get the urge to drink, take drugs, etc, use the tool of playing things forward. On that note, here's my poem.

Play Things Forward

Play things forward. It's an extremely useful tool
Things might have gone differently if they had taught you this
in school
When beer gardens look tempting, I play things forward in my
mind
The worst-case scenario after that is 'it's just one glass of wine'
I know one million percent it would never just be one
For a glass of crushed grapes, all my hard work would be
undone
Would I even find the strength again to pull myself from
despair?
For that 'one glass of wine' on all those who love me, would it
be fair?
I playthings forward and imagine all the world I've built come
crashing down
I imagine my daughter's sweet smile melting into a frown
And I think would it really be worth it
For a quick fix hit
When your friends go home after their night out
But you get the taxi driver to pull into the shop, to drink at
home on your own, no doubt
When they are in bed nursing their hangovers from the night
before
You have just woken the beast that craves so much more
Quite simply, I actually don't want it, not even in the sunshine
or on Christmas day
Because I see it like snakes and ladders, and I don't want to
play
I don't want to ever go back to the beginning of the board
With my mind as the servant corner shop as the lord
I like being in control of my thoughts and my feelings
When I say things now, they have truthful meanings
If I avoid parties or tricky situations, sometimes
It's because I have boundaries in place that get stronger with
time
Because nothing or no one would ever be worth
Me waking that dormant sleeping mind curse

My life may seem a bit boring now I don't intoxicate myself
with beer
That's because I playthings forward to my biggest fear
I would never want to compromise myself
The things that I love, my self-worth and health
I have worked too hard, lodes more work to do
Try to play things forward and see if it works for you

Chapter Five

So, What the Fuck Do I do Now?
Who Am I?

So, you're thinking about entering recovery, or you may be a few days, months, or years deep into it. It's scary to think, 'what do I do with my life now?' When everything you have ever known has revolved around drink.

Now you go to the cinemas, and it's behind the counter by the popcorn, it's in the bowling alleys, you can take a glass of wine into the wacky.

(Understandable that place is pure torture, few diazepam wouldn't go a miss in there either) jokes, I'm not promoting Valium here, sorry naughty Beth. My point is, what do you do with your life now?

In active addiction, you lose yourself, you forget your hopes and dreams, your hobbies, apart from things that involve getting steaming, obviously, and you just kind of plod along. Time speeds up as you drink the bottle. Now it feels like all you're left with is time.

You just need to learn how to fill it. Even if you watch the TV, it's going to trigger you. At the forefront of every soap, right in the heart of them, is a pub, The Vic, The Woolpack, The Rovers Return.

I couldn't even imagine sitting down to watch TV and enjoying programmes without a bottle by my side. I watched Game of Thrones intoxicated, Vikings steaming, and many series on the Tudors brandy filled.

I remember dragons, a dwarf, and some dead people with weird blue eyes, but then it all gets a bit muddled up in your mind, and suddenly good old Henry is riding a dragon sacrificing a goat (not one of his wives this time.)

I was never really watching these things. My body was, my eyes were focused on the TV, but my mind was completely elsewhere, probably bottle-watching. When you first get your bottle, you are overjoyed. You drink quite contently until you get halfway down.

Then you start to panic and begin to feel scared about running out. So, with each glass after that, you're worrying about the next one.

You don't really enjoy the one you have because you are fearful of running out. You can't really get into a series because halfway through, you'll be nipping to the shop to top up. Or you will lose your keys, phone, remote, marbles, pride, sanity and get distracted by searching for them.

I am lucky that I had an extreme love for poetry before any addiction. I have always used it as a tool to express myself, even as a child.

I put a lot of focus and energy into my poetry, into trying to build a business based on poetry to help others.

What if you loathe poetry? you can't bear to sit in front of the flickering box, and for the life of you, you can't think of a hobby or something you may find peace and enjoyment from.

Well, I would imagine that would feel very lonely.

In recovery, at first, your social circle of drinking friends and night out acquaintances get smaller.

It can feel very lonely, and I imagine it is a noticeably crucial factor in pulling people back into the drinking lifestyle.

Nobody likes to feel alone or ostracised.

Think of this, as cheesy as this may sound the world is full of natural highs that we take for granted, that we never for a second took notice of in active addiction.

I remember being about four months sober; opposite, where I lived at the time, was a park.

I got up fresh and early one Sunday morning and walked through it. For the first time in over a decade, I took notice of the smell of freshly cut grass.

I noticed the flowers popping up as it was spring, and a rabbit jumped out of nowhere, and the sight of that nature was so beautiful it brought tears to my eyes. I listened to the laughter of children playing in the park, and every sense in my body seemed to come alive. It was like an epiphany.

My Sundays before had been filled with regrets. If I was up early, it was because I was chasing the hair of the dog. I would be cooking Sunday dinner but find enjoyment more in the wine meant for the gravy juice.

Although so small and probably an everyday daily occurrence to so many people, this moment in nature blew my mind. For the first time in a long time, I've seen beauty in the world again sober, alert aware.

I was awaiting the book coming back from the publishes after being formatted this week and I got a sudden flash back of a time when my Belle was about one and a half. The week before I had been on a date with this really fit guy who had his own house business nice car etc.

I was so nervous I got absolutely steaming and during the date drank two bottles of wine. I looked and acted a mess, so he ghosted me. It was one Sunday, and I was extremely hungover, so I went to the shop in my onesie.

This was no ordinary onesie it was a monkey onesie with a swinging tail and monkey ears. I was in the shop trying to pick a quick fix to stop me feeling like utter shite. Then who do you think enters the shop fitty Ghosty Mc'Ghostyson.

I'm like fuck I'm in my monkey onesie looking like a crack head.

So, I duck down hoping he wouldn't see me, I'm on my hands and knees in my monkey onesie looking like I'd escaped from the fucking zoo.

Errrm well he did see me, and I had to pretend I was looking for something I had dropped. I'll never forget the look of horror on his face like what a nut job.

I just said to the cashier 'yep I'll just have all the vodka please' After he left.

That must have been comedy gold for that shop keeper.

My Sundays are very, different now, I don't even own a onesie anymore, maybe I could get a sheep one and go mess with the farmers heads at the back of mine and blend in with the other sheep all day on all fours then just get up and walk off when they try round them up.

Love The Most

Sundays
Used to be the worst days
Dealing with the aftermath of the weekend state
Now every Sunday, there will always be a roast on our plate
There will be uniform clean, and smelling fresh
No regrets about a weekend sesh
Just ordinary days of forest walks,
Meaningful Mother daughter talks
Ordinary days without Drama are quite delightful
The beauty in soba sleeps insightful
Rested, alert, aware
That it's still in me ingrained somewhere
So, I don't let it, even for a second, slip into my mind. I know
the sneaky style
I don't walk by the Alcohol aisle
I have built up so much that I truly love this peace
So, I Armour up to fight this beast
I take my dog for little walks on a Sunday
I embrace the thought of Monday
It doesn't send shivers down my spine
I polish the school shoes till they Shine
It's just trivial things, not massive things that normal people do
That you find joy in once again as your exploring a fresh life
new
It's not for brownie points or to gloat or boast
I don't hate Sundays anymore; in fact, I think I love them the
most

I'm not advising anyone to become an avid nature walker or write pages of poetry. I am not telling you recovery is filled with joy daily because that's unrealistic. What have you always been passionate about deep down in your heart enjoyed?

Is it dance, singing, golfing, fishing, knitting, boxing, football, or education?

The list is endless.

For so long, we filled our lives with all that was bad for us, so now, let's fill them with a bit of joy and a natural high.

The good part is when you feel joy, our bodies release endorphins, and when you go to the gym, they reward us with a natural high, so, that's a bonus.

I mentioned education.

I've enjoyed getting back into education and learning about addiction, and how the brain works. There is a recovery college online and a place I love in Birmingham called Fircroft college, which is fantastic.

There is power in knowledge, building up your mind, like if you're going to war armouring up. Addiction is a war. It is an internal battle of the mind, so what harm will it do to educate yourself on it?

In active addiction, we sometimes take jobs we don't enjoy, to pay the bills and feed the beast.

We spend most of our time working, so what is it that you want to do that will make you happy?

If you are anything like me, your mind would say 'you can't do that. Stay in your box. Who are you trying to be?'

But you can do it if you put half of the passion and drive into your new life in recovery, that you did when you were chasing that fix.

You can do anything.

We consider failures to be something awful. However, if you learn from your mistakes and grow from them, they make you wise and strong. Sobriety, recovery getting out of bed takes strength every day.

You are actively choosing to live a better, more fulfilled life. So even on days where you want to cry and can't face getting out of bed if you don't give in and don't relapse, you're still a million times better than other days when you did.

Also, if you do pick up, don't wallow in it. We are unlearning a pattern of a lifetime, don't let mistakes or relapses define who you are, dust yourself off and try again, but journal the events, feelings, and emotions that lead you to that relapse, and think to yourself what can I do next time to defend myself? learn from it. Don't beat yourself up over and over. If we learn from our failures, are they really failures?

The definition of the word insanity in the dictionary is doing the same thing over and over again and expecting a different result.

That's why addiction is insanity, but we are human. No one person's recovery journey is the same.

In fact, in recovery terms, I am just a baby. I've still very much to learn. However, while I'm learning, I wanted to share what I've learned. My methods may not work for some. They may even seem downright stupid. However, they may not, So I decided to share them anyway.

So really, the point of this chapter is that in recovery, it's a bit like you're re-learning everything again. Even in my case, how to love in an adult manner, how to be kind to myself, how to give less fucks about people's opinions.

Find the thing that works for you, no matter what it is. If it brings you joy, try it. Not promoting anything illegal or unsafe here, just thought I'd put that out there so I can't get blamed should anyone enjoy that kind of activity. No judgments, but let's try to keep it upbeat.

If necessary, list possible things and try them all to find your thing for you.

Try lots of recovery methods until ...

One works. If NA OR AA is not your thing, try SMART Recovery, and join Facebook support groups with Google, the world's your oyster just do not carry the weight alone. Most importantly, when you tell yourself you can't, tell yourself you can, so here's a poem of empowerment I wrote.

Warrior Woman

It's so easy to pick yourself apart when you look in the mirror
Not seeing the warrior, you are and focusing on wanting to be
thinner
It's easy to distract yourself from your hopes and dreams
Reading about the latest celebrity's weight loss in gossip
magazines
Why do I need to know this woman's weight or even her age?
As you read about them modifying their bodies on every page
To fit inside the box of stereotypical beauty
What about values and beliefs, no that's boring reading, you see
We forget that our bodies gave birth
We placed another human on this earth
We put ourselves down and don't build ourselves up
Not seeing the beauty in our brains, just the way that we look
We analyse situations and think it's something we did wrong
As though we are listening to on repeat some kind of self-doubt
song
We fall back when in pain and hide from the hurt
We forget all our qualities, even our self-worth
Remember, though, all you have been through and where you
stand now!
Like a mantra in your head and repeat it somehow
I am worth it; I am strong, I am brave, I am kind
Play it on repeat, so it sticks in your mind
Put yourself first. Place yourself upon the pedal stall
Pick yourself up, dust yourself off when you fall
Learn lessons from it and use it as your drive
Fuel for you fires a tool to survive
Remember that you are more than just skin, and you are more
than just bone
Love yourself and who you are when you're feeling alone
If ever you're feeling self-doubt or you're a little bit lost
Remember, you're a survivor of internal wars and hit your day
like a boss

Sit With Me

When the coldest wind is blowing within the depth of the
storm,
It will pass, and the winds will turn into a breeze that blows soft
and warm
I know the road seems far too winding to even attempt to walk
So don't think of that road right now, we can sit in silence, or
we can sit and talk
Just know that what seems unfixable will find a way to mend
One day a stranger you haven't met yet will be your dearest
friend
Please don't close your eyes yet; all is not lost
There Is a sun hiding behind the clouds that can melt through
the thickest frost
It's just far too hard to see right now when the clouds are far
too black
There is a way forward, so please stop looking back
Our minds can create things that aren't even real
Time is there to mend broken wounds, at least try to help them
to heal
Please understand this is not the twilight zone
There is no reason anyone should suffer in silence, to ever feel
alone
Please dial my number. I will talk to you
Never mock or judge what you're going through
I know the pain is overwhelming, like those thoughts within
your mind
Although it's hard to see yourself, to yourself you should be
kind,
Scream if you must let it all out
Things will get better, I know, I promise I KNOW. I have no
doubt

Chapter Six

Things I Have Done That Have Helped Me (Visual)

I started marking my days green for sober days. My dad brought me a Tom Hardy calendar, the first sober Christmas I had. That visual representation of keeping the days green has become part of my daily routine. It's now a peaky blinders calendar, aha.

The first month of doing this really helped because the thought of going to the calendar and putting a massive red line through it was something I did not want to do. In active addiction, we unknowingly hide the addiction, even from ourselves, the empty bottles stashed under the sink, the out-of-sight, out-of-mind approach. I remember when I moved, clearing under the sink, and finding lots, and I mean lots, of empty bottles.

Bottles of vodka, brandy, cheap rum. I lived on my own, well, with my daughter, but she was too young to understand.

I remember thinking,

From whom was I hiding these bottles?

(Ok so word changed that to, from whom I don't bloody talk like that but, I like it though, I imagine a posh person being like 'whom on earth was one hiding one's champagne bottles from')

I then realised it must have been from myself.

However, you cannot hide an extensive red line on the calendar, and who could lie to Tom Hardy's face?

I didn't want to lie to the calendar, and I didn't want to have to lie to Tom either, so those green days turned into months which turned into a year, and then so on, and that first calendar hangs proudly in the little office space I carved out for myself in my room.

Tom Hardy is in recovery, which helped him feel relatable, as is Eminem and many other famous people now.

People who have achieved extraordinary things in their life despite their addiction.

They did not let their addiction define them. They used it as fire to succeed and thrive, which helped me think I could do that too.

If you actively research famous people in addiction, it may help you find strength.

It may help you feel less alone. It did for me, that's for sure.

On that note, music really helped me. I found artists in recovery and listened to their music; every word in their songs hit a little harder.

When us girls was younger my dad used to have a strange taste in music, and we came across this album he had of this guy called Rufus Wainwright. He had this song called 'oh What a world.

It had a big, massive orchestra playing in it and we would get really stoned and stomp about to it. If you need a quick pick me up, you can't not feel happy after hearing that song.

Kelly Clarkson got me through so many break ups. The Girls used to come round mine we would all for some reason get our baps out do air guitar and sing now that your gone. Felt really empowering.

Tom Mc Donald his very controversial and I don't agree with everything he says but some of his songs really hit hard. James Arther Recovery Song.

When feeling down, I would listen to music and absorb myself into it, listening to every word. During one of the lockdowns, I would just put my earphones in and walk in nature, which became a little daily buzz. I authored a poem about it.

Here it is, it's called I put my earphones in.

I PUT MY EARPHONES IN

I put my earphones in and blast my worries away
I just walk and walk till I feel ok
I close my eyes breathe the air in, and listen to the music
Remind myself this is just a moment in time and that I can do
this
The man-made pool is closed can't swim, and the mind
becomes a hater
So, I reminded myself I still have legs, and I'm blessed with
mother nature
Each step that I take is like my mind is emptying like its sifting
flour
Putting my mind back on track taking control, and the power
Each foot in front of the other removes toxic thoughts from my
head
So, they don't come out to play when I'm lying in bed
I listen to Mya case of the ex, mockingbird black-eyed peas
Listening to where is the love while I'm surrounded by trees
I listen to anything that puts a little fire in my soul
I walk, and I walk until I reach an end goal
This could be a conclusion in my mind or clarity of some sort
I walk; still, I walk never cut my mind short
You see, I need to clear this messy mind of mine
So, I put my earphones in come rain or shine
If I don't, things build up and pile on, and my mind goes into a
jumble
So, I walk close my eyes, and I sift through the jungle
So easy to go down a harmful route and get lost with no way
out
So, I walk away from any fear, and I play music through my
doubt
Whatever it is that is playing on my mind
I walk earphones in till it's the peace that I find

I also a few months in exposed myself as such on social media. I had spent so many years hiding from myself that I wanted to become authentic and truthful and try to help struggling others. The words of encouragement helped me tremendously. We spent so much time lying to everyone about everything. When we are stuck in the cycle, honesty is like a breath of fresh air.

I am not recommending that you do this. You may rather stay private, or if you expose yourself, it may negatively affect your job, family life etc.

Only you know yourself and your story and what is suitable for you. However, in the last few years, so many people have reached out to me, which is one of the reasons I have authored this book.

People can be selfish with things, and one thing people can be selfish with is knowledge, people don't share it in fear it might kick start people to succeed more than them.

I like to share anything I learn, which may help someone, because I know what it feels like to be in so much pain you do not want to live. If I can help in easing someone's pain, then I will.

I will admit though it is rewarding, not like when you buy a homeless man a sandwich, take a picture of it, and put it on social media rewarding, I hate it when people do that.

But rewarding in the sense that I won't tell anyone else the story these people might have told me, but it brings me so much joy that I can help other people with advice and things I've learned.

It makes it feel like it wasn't there in vain, my addiction, yes, I made terrible choices, but now other people can receive help from the good ones I've made.

I can relate with empathy to people's bad choices because I've made them too, so I can understand.

However, it could be hurtful when you keep trying to help someone, and they throw your kindness back in your face.

In helping others, you must protect yourself. All you can do is give advice. If that advice isn't taken the 3rd, 4th, or 5th time you must step back.

This has helped me to realise what it must have felt like for my friends and family seeing me destroy myself and know the solution there in black and white that I just couldn't see.

So, I now understand why they were so frustrated, but at the time, I just had resentment for them for not seeing my pain.

Seeing someone, you love destroying themselves in front of your eyes must have been awful for them. I could not see that then, but now I do, and I understand why some of those people had to take a step back from me at the time.

I've built back so many broken bridges, and if you feel like there are bridges you may have destroyed that will never be mended, believe me, they can. It just takes time.

Routine is vital to keeping you focused. Initially, the clock seems to just standstill, but you fill your days with tiny little positive things.

Don't feel pressured to go back to work until you feel well enough to do so.

Pressure is a magnitude of a force that can trigger all triggers, and then you drown in a sea of them.

We feel at first like we have something to prove, and the definition of being well is the 9 to 5 grind.

It took us years to reach the breaking point of recovery, so after a 30-day rehab stay, we're not necessarily going to be fighting fit to take on the world.

You learn new things about yourself daily, and we are relearning what you thought you knew.

Even our taste buds change, we have started to find our identity again.

We crave sugar like you couldn't imagine. That's because alcohol is loaded with sugar. It's called the recovery cake belly.

So, you may experiment with hair dye, clothes etc.

It's like a breakup when you want to wash that man straight out of your hair.

The reflection changes. You start to see yourself sober for the first time in years, and suddenly, you want to start caring for yourself.

That opened a newfound addiction to face cream, an obsession with face masks, perfumes, makeup, and fancy creams.

Suppose we always just find a cross-addiction. It seeps through somewhere, excepting it is ingrained in us, and finding the ability to laugh at the insanity of it sometimes can take the pressure off.

When you fixate on something, pause, and think, 'I know what's going on here, you, sneaky little fucker', or just purchase it if it doesn't harm you or your finances.

Is that good advice?

I don't know, but when we give up all the naughty stuff, will it kill us having shit lodes of shit we don't need just to quieten our head? No, it's not. We need to do the work, too, of course, but as far as I know, no one has ever died of having too many trainers or a face cream addiction.

If we are not doing it to escape or fix feelings, as they call it, and every time you feel slightly sad, you run to amazon like a bull in a China shop.

Colour co ordinating become a bit of a thing too.

I know why I do it. It's because I have found a little self-love inside, and I want that to reflect on the outside.

But it can be an expensive game. I acknowledge it and try to keep an eye on it. My skin looks absolutely fabulous. (Or does it maybe I need some of that brand new stuff that makes u look 20, or the latest slimming pill u take and wake up 2 stone lighter aha)

Anti-Wrinkle Cream

I collect anti-wrinkle cream and cleanse and tone my skin every
night
Nothing to boast about or be frilled about, right
Well, to me it really is it's part of a self-care routine
Cause let's face it, people in active addiction are not known for
being clean.
Mud masks and hair oils honestly fill me with joy
When I'm in boots, it's like Christmas. I'm like a kid with a toy
When you spent most of your adult life in oblivion, you don't
really care for clean skin
You're not going to cleanse the outside while you intoxicate
from within.
You don't pay your bills, let alone buy pretty things for
yourself
You prioritise vodka above heating your house
Now I pay my bills every single one
I collect wax melts and cleaning items just for fun.
When you lived life with the Tasmanian devil in your head
Spinning around till the addiction gets fed
You find solace in those tiny things, a clean house, face, and
fresh sheets
Do you like your cushions a certain way placed, tidy and neat?
It's not because you are trying to be something you are not
You know where you came from. You have never forgot
It's just it's much happier here in the peace with the fancy
shampoo
No longer burn marks on the heels of your shoe
From when you hot foot marched to the shop early doors
You like cleaning your home, no longer see it as tedious chores
It's about a tidy house, tidy mind, clean face, clean soul
I don't like to not do these things because it's a slippery hole
I like to buy myself Anti-wrinkle cream
Keep the side of my street tidy and clean
So, if people throw mud, it does not stick
Or if it ever does, ill cleanse and tone it off quick

Do you really need that?
I went to clean my teeth and realised I have seven different
types of toothpaste
I can't go into a shop now without getting a new cream or
serum for my face
My bathtub is scattered with several types of shampoo
I get anxious when they are not full to the top, so I buy a fresh
one new
I must have my cushions placed a certain way
I have a ritual I do now at the end of the day
I get in bed after making sure everything is off n double-locking
the door
I lie down, get comfortable then must check once more
I think the face cream fasciation started when I started
practicing a little self-care
I must get another one although I don't need another one, I've
got plenty I'm aware
But it gives me a little buzz
In the same way, getting amazon parcels does
I mean, like you would think, I'd be loaded not drinking every
week
But not really when I must buy that new serum from Clinique
I'm not trying to boast about excellent brands here
More trying to explain how fixations cost you dear
It's not the same, obviously, as intoxicating yourself
It's buying 10 different types of disinfectant to clean your
house.
I think it comes from the old days of living in chaos and my
skin feeling transparent and dry
Self-soothing in a way, or at least that's what I say at the till as
I buy
Cross-addictions happen to the best of us
When I'm in boots, I feel like a kid at toys are us
I love putting my makeup on and making myself feel glam
Changing my face for whoever it is that day, I'm embracing
that I am
I like to smell of fragrance strong and sweet
Not like brandy and regret and cheesy feet
From when the alcohol would sweat from my skin

I take vitamins now to feel good from within
I know a face cream obsession is not going to kill me neither
will disinfecting my house
Friends in recovery, do you get the same compulsive
obsessions?
I'd love to hear the ones of everyone else

Try visual things to help mark the days. There are also lots of apps, and stuff from Google Play. Check them out and see if one suits you.

Or not to put too much pressure on yourself. Trust me, I know how hard that can be.

If you find that bit of self-love, embrace it.

Go onto you tube and type in sound baths thank me for it later oh it's beautiful. I typed up this book listening to focus music on you tube to stop my busy mind.

Face masks, bubble baths, candles, and tunes of your choice can be heavenly.

It doesn't need to be fancy creams if we sound nice and present nice, even if that's just brushing our hair, cleaning our teeth, and putting a fresh pair of knickers on.

Subconsciously we present ourselves with more confidence because we feel more self-worth.

I go places now without make up on. I prefer it if I have it on if I am honest because it feels like my war paint as such, but I don't feel like it is the end of the world if I nip to the shops without any on now.

So, we don't need to rely on that mask of a Brandy boost that gives us goggle eyes when we see ourselves in the mirror because that reflection is inaccurate and not what other people see.

Wish For Any Thing

If I could wish for anything apart from peace on earth
It would be for the girl with lonely eyes to understand her worth
It would be for all that is bad to just turn into rainbow
butterflies
That would wipe away the tears she cries
To help the man with greasy hair reaching for his pipe
Realise he's not old and rotten and that his soul could still be
ripe
If only he could fight his demons, troubles, and toil
Walk away from those squats and shiny foil
What about that lady sitting on the edge, tears pouring
Who has finally cracked all the pain she has been ignoring?
Well, I could hold out my hand
Help her to find her grief, help her try to understand
Those bad things can happen to good people
And that, unfortunately, we were not all born equal
So, the old lady who is cold and desperate for some heat
Having to choose between warmth or something to eat
My wish would be to help them all
Not a big gesture, something tiny and small
Something that may seem to others irrelevant
But to that person in a hole can be seen as evidence
Those things can change; a smile in a crowd can save a
person's life
I'd love to pull them out of the darkness and back into the light

Turning Negative Situations into Positive Ones and Not Dwelling on Them

Remember before I said I've had covid for a couple of weeks. This meant my daughter, dog, and I had stayed in our abode for two weeks other than to go to the bins.

Not put makeup on, and my daughter is practically moulded into a Unicorn onesie. I went for a glorious pair of Winnie the Pooh bottoms.

Anyhow, it's been a bit shitty, I will admit.

More than anything, I've missed my sense of smell and taste. These would seem like simple things that we take for granted, but not being able to smell your morning coffee or the food you eat makes life a little joyless.

However, my sense of smell has returned today, and I am so grateful for it.

Sometimes we must lose the things we have taken for gospel to realise how much they mean to us.

My morning coffee this morning was heavenly. It literally tasted like magic.

Now, I will take note more of my surroundings.

You know when a posh lady walks past you, and you get that whiff of her perfume, and you imagine her home would look like a show home, and she probably makes bread from scratch.

Or when you're walking down the street, and you smell home cooking or freshly cut grass (even though I have hay fever and my eyes swell up like golf balls in the summer)

I'm going to notice these things more. It may last a week, but it might be me, if you see a woman walking down the street sniffing random stuff like a dog.

Would I have had the chance to sit down and write these chapters in this book if I was doing school runs, workshops, meetings, and all the other stuff that quickly fills up the week? (Probably not)

I'm not saying it's been all fun and games because it hasn't. My body is taken a bit of a beating, but I can still take positives from this situation instead of being like why me.

Sometimes the question should be, why not me?

You could take this kind of thinking into anything; sometimes, I can feel at times in life I have impostor syndrome.

Especially when I am doing something positive. I've been learning to drive. It's a rollercoaster of emotions.

Some weeks I could move from A to B without overwhelming anxiety, and everything went smoothly. Other weeks I'm like, 'BETH, you're behind the wheel of a car, you're driving, you can't do this, you're going to crash, you probably going to cause a major incident etc.'

Then it's like I lose the ability to do simple tasks I know how to do.

I overtalk when I'm nervous. I started talking to my driving instructor about a job I'd seen on gumtree once when a man offered £50 for you to throw custard at him. I was like, 'I really wish I took that job. I think it would have been fun.'

Luckily, he's a funny man, saying things like, 'Beth I would have thrown custard on him for £50.'

I bet he goes home and says to his Mrs. 'I had that loon again today.'

My point is, yes, I went off track. I do, do that. Unlike before, when I have a lousy week driving, I try to learn from my mistakes by going to the new lesson with a clean slate.

I realised one time I forgot to eat beforehand, so I was particularly hangry. You know that word when we mix hungry and angry together (words having a bitchfit over it because it's not in the dictionary)

In turn, which amplified my anxiety. We underestimate the power of simple things.

Am I tired?

Am I hungry?

Am I thirsty?

Am I emotional or hormonal?

These things all play their parts in our mood, so now I try and make an emotional infantry tick list, before I must do important things, so they don't contribute to my life negatively.

The same method of learning from mistakes can go with failed relationships.

There could be mitigating factors, like drinking, drugs, cheating, or being at different points in life.

These can lead to the breakdown of a relationship.

I have learned that one of the biggest things is more communication. So now, instead of dwelling on relationships that have not panned out. I have realised they didn't work out for a reason.

Does not mean all the blame lies with them, or it all lies with me. It could be one of those things. They have their truth; I have my truth, and somewhere in the middle is what happened, it can only be about perspectives, really.

I have realised I used to take all the negative traits of one relationship into a new one. We could be in relationships with ten different people, but it's just the same relationship, going after the same type of person.

Bad boys, the ones you want to save, then cry when they mistreat you.

Really it was an ego thing, that you thought you could change them, that they would love you so much they would stop their wayward ways. You can't dip your toes in the ocean and then cry when they get wet.

So easy to put people on a pedal stool, to only see the good in them when your gut is literally screaming at you, and the red flags are flying everywhere. Listen to your own intuition. It is telling you something for a reason.

You can't save everybody, and even if your intentions are from kindness, remember primarily to be kind to yourself.

If one method has yet to work out for you, dissect it.

Why do you make these choices?

Does it go back to the comfort in pain thing?

Or is it because it's dangerous and exciting, that we are thrill seekers?

I'm not saying settle for anyone. You know your type and what ticks your boxes, but maybe just think can I imagine myself with this person in five years or is this a temporary fix for loneliness and sexual desire.

If that is what it is and you don't want anything more serious, that's ok too. Just make sure it's what you want or that you and whoever is on your mind at the minute, are singing from the same hymn sheet and on the same page.

I'm no love guru. Over the years, I've made poor choices and undersold myself and my self-worth significantly.

I have given my heart to people that gave no shit about breaking it, and I have hurt people that would have probably treated me well.

Do you want to know a little nugget of a gift that recovery has given me?

Some of my exes or people I have been intertwined with over the years have reached out to me since I've been sober for a while.

They said they were proud of me and then went on to ask for help, which I gladly gave them.

I have given them this help even if they mistreated me in the past because I am going by the merit of who they are now.

Not who they were while stuck in the cycle. Who they are now is someone reaching out for help, acknowledging I've worked hard to stay sober, and trying to better themselves. That must be tough to reach out to an ex, and I respect and admire that.

I will help anyone who truly wants to better themselves. But I do it with healthy boundaries. I can't save everyone or get sucked into being emotionally involved because that may hinder my recovery, or my beautiful relationship with my wonderful partner.

When I enter a relationship now, I do it with caution. I will love, but never to the level I used to let myself love because that was toxic.

It is a protection process.

It also helps to know if something does not work out in the future, it can't break me. It will hurt me. I'll be sad for a while, but I'll return from it more robust than before.

That's the beauty of being hurt so badly in the past. Everything else can feel like a walk in the park.

In that sense, my past mistakes protect me from the heartbreak of the future, so we have it a negative situation turned into a positive one.

THE BOOK

If you were to read a book, you wouldn't just skip a chapter
Although everybody wants to get to the part that reads happy
ever after
There will be sentences, paragraphs, and pages
Reflecting on difficulties and the different life stages
If we didn't know pain, we wouldn't know love
If we didn't know bad, then we couldn't know good
Ying and Yang positive and negative
Learning to grow is learning to forgive
The rain makes us sad, but the rain helps things grow
You must weather the storm before blossoming flowers show
You see, to flourish truly, the flowers must get fed
It's the same as the mind that resides in our head
If we only concentrate on the negative
It becomes toxic
Toxicity equally equals negativity
Positiveness isn't always easy
If you let it though, it can be
Easily incorporated into a daily routine
Giving you the ability to believe in an (impossible) dream
So, no point in skimming or flipping through the page
Fast forward the clock to old age
One day that chapter that you wanted to skip
With reflection can be the making of all of it

Take My Light

The bruises may not be physically laid upon my body or my
face
But the bruises lie within my mind triggered by a sound, a
smell, a place
I could be walking along minding my own business, then a
flashback comes to me
That causes a dip in the mental frame and induces the PTSD
I may not have black eyes or broken bones or a broken jaw
But the bruises seep into my mind at night, and they make my
head feel sore
They come in the forms of nightmares, and they come in the
form of fears
Yet I am far too strong a person now to let the bruises release
my tears
Doesn't matter how many years pass. The words can replay on
repeat
Your fat, your ugly, and no one wants you. That's the reason
why I cheat
Although I know I'm far more now than what's on the outside
My ego took a smash, and to ashes went my pride
It's like you're building a new home now, but every now and
then, someone steals the bricks
It's like you're writing out daily chores, and someone's putting
crosses by your ticks
But you keep on fighting, though, you defeated the dreaded
drink
So how come, after years of freedom, he can still hurt the way
you think
Who knows if it will ever truly go away
I do, I know that for every bad word, there will be a positive
one I say
On the whole, that is getting easier, and I'm growing and
thriving more and more
But when the flashbacks hit me hard of, cowering on the floor
I forget that I'm a warrior a strong independent fighter
You may have attacked my dreams before, yet I'm still a book
writer

And I will keep on writing until one day, this weight lifts
Because you may have tried to take my spirit, but it's one of my
strongest gifts
So, when it came back, it empowered me to take back the pen
and write
So, you sit in your darkness because I've taken back my light

Chapter Seven

The Storm

Today was my first day out of Isolation, I went to Asda, and it didn't fill me with the usual level of anxiety I get. I was glad to be active. I love seeing other people going about their business and getting to pick fresh food I could cook.

It felt so lovely to put some makeup on again, and wear actual clothes, not jogging bottoms.

Last night though, there was a massive storm. There were many broken branches and tired-looking trees on the car journey.

It was quite a scary storm; I had my daughter and dog in bed. Last night my daughter was scared, so I hugged her till she fell asleep. The roof sounded like it would blow off, but we felt safe in our bed in our little haven and knew the storm would pass.

It took me back to when I was about four months into recovery.

We still lived in Birmingham at the time. My daughter stayed out for the night at her Dads Mom's. It was a bad storm, with thunder and lightning, and I was home with just my dog.

My phone rang, and it was my beautiful daughter 'Hello, Mommy, are you ok? I have been worried about you in the storm. I hope you are not scared. I love you, Mommy. I just wanted to make sure you were ok.'

It warmed my heart more than I could ever describe at the time. She must have only been about eight. Instead of having fun with her Nan she couldn't sleep because she was worried about me being ok in the storm.

I thought last night, 'I wonder how many times my innocent little girl worried about me' For years, my whole life has been like a storm. One blown down branch after another, as I was about to go down that rabbit hole of memory lane beating myself about all my past mistakes, I brought myself back to the here and now. Right here, at this moment, I am protecting her just as I should be. I am her haven now. She can fall asleep in my arms, knowing tomorrow the storm will pass. right here in this bed in our little castle, we are at peace.

Castle in the Sky

We live in a flat my daughter, my dog, and I
But to us, it's our very own castle in the sky
It's only two floors up, but when we close the door
My bed can be a pirate ship surrounded by the sea, swishing
carpet on the floor
When we close the door, it can be anything
No longer a bed but a wrestling ring
We can make dens, and I can cuddle up to my dependents
We can put on the Disney channel and watch the descendants
We hear bearing from the sheep from our place
Wherever we are in the world, it will be home, if I can see their
face
We read stories at night time a few pages or so
It warms my heart more than she could ever know
To live in such a beautiful part of the world, I feel so lucky for
this fresh start
I can be known here as only who I am now, who I always was
deep down in my heart
Not a wreck or drunken swirling tornado of trouble
Some days I fear something may pop this bubble
I've never felt this before, happy and content
Every bill is paid on time no worries about rent
Our home is a home now that has only ever known this version
of us
Not walls that were filled with dreams that were crushed
Moving here was the best choice I have made for my little
family
I feel as though it's opened doors to newfound creativity
It's quieter here. Things move at a different pace
My daughter, my dog, and I, our castle in the sky, our very own
perfect safe space

Once she was asleep, my mind regressed down memory lane. It attacked me with childhood memories and things I had not considered for years.

My mind spun around like a washing machine. It reminded me of all those painful nights I would wake up at 2:00 in the morning and torture myself for hours upon hours on end. I remembered how it felt to feel like you're the only person awake in the world.

To itch all over as the alcohol poured out of your body sweat. I remember the 2:00 am back-and-forth conversations where I would say not today. I will be sober today because I cannot have another night like this.

I hated myself so much I couldn't bear to look in the mirror. I would after I pilled on shit loads of makeup. I might have even taken a pissed-up selfie. Now I have looked back at some of those selfies, and there is nothing but pain in my eyes. You can't cover that up with makeup.

I haven't had a night like this in a long time. It may have been because we have been stuck on Groundhog Day for the last two weeks, not really doing much with our time but being under the weather. Therefore, we only created a few memories. We never used our brains that much. We had no other human interaction. Hardly any exercise. I had gone from doing 12,000 steps most days on the school run to barely hitting five hundred around flat.

So, my mind decided to regurgitate old memories to get them ticking again. Adding the cherry on top of the cake gave me some glorious nightmares.

However, today is a new day, and I have processed it. I understand why my mind did it, so I will not let it ruin my night-time routine tonight.

I love my sleep.

My friends in the winter call me Beth the bear, because I want to sleep when it is dark outside.

Being in recovery, our sleep is so different. It's not a drunken slumber. It's actual sleep. Most nights, if I must be up at 6:00 am, I will go to bed at 9, knowing it will take me about an hour to drop off.

(I've been going a bit crazy lately, staying up till 10, sometimes even half past. I know, wild, right)

I need a solid 8 hours to function. It's caused relationship problems before my early bedtime routine, but I know my body, and I know it will negatively affect my next day if I don't get enough sleep. So, I'm not going to stop doing it.

I love dreaming, not the drinking dreams they do my head in, but they don't hurt me like they used to. Dreaming fascinates me that your mind creates all these things. It's like watching your very own movie inside your head. I trust my dreams, too, because sometimes they give me muddled messages or show me things I did not even know were on my mind. I also have a night-time routine now.

Back to all those lotions and potions I told you about before. It makes me feel great putting on my makeup mask in the morning to face the day. It also makes me feel great at night, washing it off, cleansing and toning my skin, putting on my night-time cream and feeling fresh, and going to sleep with brushed teeth.

My daughter jokes and calls me creamy Beth because I now put so much face cream on. I think I do it because in a drunken slumber, I was not washing my makeup off, let alone creaming up my skin, and my breath was more tones of brandy than mouthwash. So, when I'd go to the mirror in the morning with panda eyes and a breath that could melt a hole through metal, it was more of a 'for fuck's sake' moment than 'I'm going to embrace the day.'

They sound like such tiny trivial things, but they make a difference.

Wash up if there are any plates in the sink, so they don't pile up. Clean the kitchen sides, so I do not have to do it in the morning. Or when I wake up, the sight of it puts me in a bad mood.

I'm no Mrs Finch. I can be messy, and my home is lived in and not for show, but these tiny little things all make my mind less messy. My washing smells like fairy softener because I'm heavy-handed with it.

I love the smell. I try not to let the laundry pile get too much, or the wardrobes get too messy because when they do, I know my mental health is declining. So, I check in on these things.

Here's my poem Wrinkles. ▨

Wrinkles

One day if I am lucky enough my face will be filled with lines
and wrinkles
The same face that once had adolescent pimples
My eyes will though always remain the same
Sometimes blue and bright in love or cloudy in pain
If I am lucky enough, this body of mine will age
I am on the 30th chapter and am currently putting ink on that
page
It would be a blessing to see other decades pile candles upon
the cake
I saw it differently before, fearing age was a mistake
For each day that I am gifted is a blessing, not a given, to get to
live to be old
Each moment of love I have felt in my heart is a secret story to
never be told
They are precious, and time is valuable even when we fear the
clock
We should be grateful to watch it turn with age. For some they
witnessed it stop
So, if the lines on my face are made from laughter, and the
crow's feet deepen with tears
I will touch my lines and count my blessings, for they will
show the gift of the years
I wanted to love and be loved; I have that when I see my
daughter's face
I've been guilty of wishing the days away before like I was in
some kind of race
Now I even cherish the nothing days when there is not all that
much going on
Because they are the days when I get to lie and be still to
simply just be someone's mom
I am sure she will be the cause of some of my lines, the ones
that run deep
She is the reason I wake up blessed and the peace that I get
when I sleep
I don't know if I will have other children, and I don't know
how that story will play out

All I know is I am blessed a thousand times, so I would love
them without any doubt
If they, too, added to the lines that, in time, were placed on my
face
I would cherish those lines and be grateful for the time and treat
them with much love and grace

A HAIR OF THE DOG

A Hair of the dog
At what point did it stop being one drink to another day
robbed?
Waking up with an unsatisfactory hunger
Flashing lightning in mind and roaring thunder
That will not stop; no way can you calm this storm
Did you think of a drink before your morning yawn?
Do you need it to remove the thought of last night's mistakes?
Need to consume some vodka before your cornflakes?
Just one drink, though, to take the Horrors away
Then before you know it, you're half a bottle deep. Its only
Midday
Saturdays and Sunday's blend into one another
Cooking the Sunday roast, washing the uniforms, trying to be a
good Mother
Of course, you adore your child, worth their weight in gold
It was only going to be the hair of the dog, that's how it got
sold
To yourself, you had no intention of bottle-watching that day
Drowning in housework as the day slips away
Chopping onions, singing to Amy Winehouse Rehab if only
you knew then the Irony
Nah, I haven't got a problem. No way not me
I'm a support worker. My role is to help others
Thinking back to last night, another gulp to take away the
shudders
Before you know it, you're in a cycle. It's a daily habit
Trapped in the headlights, just like that rabbit
You want to be a better person. You just don't know how to
stop this mindset thinking
At what point did that hair of the dog become just another day
drinking?

VIDEO GAME

Sometimes I feel like this world is like a video game
The same street, the same faces, everything looks the same
Then one day, you hit another level, and everything has
changed
The streets and faces all look deranged
You walk past people and don't even notice them
Then they appear in your dreams
And everything is exactly as it should be,
From their eye colour down to their faded jeans,
Moods change, buildings get knocked down
Your memories get knocked down with them, so smiles are
now frowns
And the people who meant so much to you yesterday fade into
the background
And sometimes you can be in a crowd but feel like no one's
around
People who are meant to be a part of your life stay with you
And when you mess up, they will forgive you
I suppose everyone is given choices; it depends on which ones
you choose
Strangers can become your best friends, your loved ones you
can lose
Paths are there for you to follow
Hearts are there for you to borrow
Taking the wrong path may lead to sorrow
Your whole heart can become hollow
But take the right path, and you can achieve great things
And I don't mean fancy cars and diamond rings,
I mean a feeling of accomplishment to know that you have
achieved
I mean a sense of humbleness after you have grieved
Times a healer apparently, the clock heals all pain
And all of those black clouds fall down in the rain
Move forward, head held high till you reach the next stage
Keep moving so in time you can write the next page
Never look back with regret
And the people you forget, you forgot for a reason

It just means that you didn't need them
And fuel their jealousy with success, yes feed them
Sometimes I feel like life is like a video game
Same streets, same face, everything is the same
I took the wrong path, oh, what a shame
I guess I'll just have to play that level again

£4.49

I went to the counter and asked the lady the time
I was distracted from the clock by another quarter, only 4.59
Then I remembered the bottle wasn't any business of mine
Just a quarter my head said, but I passed the thought back to the
end of the line
I left the shop and thought it only cost 4.59 to ruin my life
Cheap in pounds but heavy in price
I reverted my mind back to that cold, sharp knife
That I grasped in my hands on my darkest of night
I thought, what would it take to ever want to go back?
To carry the weight of the world on my shoulders in a
translucent sack
With no self-worth or hope reputation far from intact, being a
prisoner to that evil red cap
Why would I when this bag that I've been carrying has been
getting unpacked?
I don't drink because I don't like it. I liked it far too much
I wanted to drink until I was numb to the human touch
I craved every drop, a fountain of wine not even enough
Like a volcano bubbling till it all erupts
Last year I wanted to dig myself a hole and hide under a rock
While the advertisements showed happy families being merry,
it's like it was constant non-stop
Brandy, vodka, anything all that I couldn't have I just wanted
the whole fucking lot
Until I realised if you obsess about what you can't have, then
you will lose the plot
SO, I LEFT THE SHOP
I untied my dog and put my earphones in
My pocket was empty. There was nothing within
Not even that delightful-looking bottle of slow gin
Tomorrow I wouldn't need to be searching for dregs in the bin
It might seem like nothing at all, but to me, it was another day
done with an almighty WIN

Skin Stereotypes

Everybody at some point would have been put into a stereotype
I have been guilty of doing it to others at moments in my life
It's human nature to place other humans into this box
I would never date a man who wears sandals with socks
Like you could have just got rid of a perfect Mr
Just because he is wearing socks because he has got a blister
Or thinking someone tattooed and pierced is going to rob your
Nan
But then realising actually they are really a pleasant woman or
man
Dictated by area codes like the North and south of Solihull, a
clear divide
Paying for postcodes because posh postcodes bring pride
People cannot really help where their mother gave birth
Some of these people who are deemed miss fits are actually the
salt of the earth
We give people labels, and people buy labels to be labelled as
someone with money
But their credit card is maxed out, and payday comes and goes
like British weather when Sunny
Take a recovery meeting, for example. Sometimes when people
mention their addiction, it leaves me in shock
Because I've got a stereotypical image in my mind, and I'm
like, what the fuck
Then I feel guilty for assuming this stereotypical picture of
addiction, and I forget that was once me
Who could have been given labels like drunken Alki
So, I should be
Less assuming with these stereotypes
Because we all have a story, and who's to say which path is
right
The person with all the tattoos may be masking their pain or
covering track marks that were placed on their veins
The guy who's in sandals may be because his feet swelled up
withdrawing, and his just in pain
So, let's not put people in boxes and judge others

Because the clothes and skin that we wear are simply our
bodies covers

Chapter Eight

Bridgnorth

One of the poems talks of where I would like to live, and currently, I live in a beautiful place called Bridgnorth. I followed my dad down here. When I used to live in Birmingham and get myself into weekly disasters when things got bad, he would have to get me, Belle and pancake our dog and drive us back to Bridgnorth.

My Dad lives in a cabin in the woods and countryside a million miles away from the council estate I lived in and the hustle of bustle of Birmingham.

I've always been a Daddies girl, and I think it hit me hard when he moved. I'm glad he did now.

If he had to get me, it would have been because I was in the aftermath of an almighty bender. Sometimes on that car journey, I would cry from Birmingham to Bridgnorth.

I can remember all the feelings like they were yesterday, how warm the tears would feel as they dripped down my face. How I'd smell and how my daughter would hug me all the way, usually saying, 'it will be ok, Mommy.'

My Dad is kind and generous, funny at the most inappropriate moments, which makes it even more amusing, and he loves a row on a Karen.

We sometimes clash because we are so alike, but I would be lost without him. Even though he is ginger, he is alright. (All the fiery gingers don't get coming for me with pitchforks; I have ginger skin too, and I love my freckles)

Bridgnorth was my haven. I used to feel completely free and at peace here. My daughter would just run around so happy and gleeful.

I was still so poorly, though. At any opportunity I could get, I would try to sneak alcohol. By my dad's cabin is a big lake, you can see hares and pheasants. Unlike where I lived before (it was more like rats and peasants, and I was one of the worst.)

Drinking alone is like throwing a dart to the wind and wondering where it will land. You drink to find peace from your busy head, but it is far from peace. It is a vicious cycle that pulls you apart limb by limb. You don't even want it anymore, but you rely on it to do daily things, because your nerves are ripped to shreds without it.

I can write this now because I can see it from the outside looking in. I am so lucky that at the age of 34 just turned 35 (the deadline for the book) I have found some inner peace. Some people never actually get to that point, or they get little glimpses here and there but are dragged back in.

For anyone without knowledge of how the addictive brain works or the life experience of living with it, the solution is so simple it is there in black and white. But it simply does not work that way.

When I left Birmingham, I left behind everything I had ever known to a place I did not know, but I needed to do it. I needed to change everything. This doesn't have to be the only solution, but it was something that worked for me.

When I started writing this book, I was going to call it snakes and ladders, which is basically about the ups and downs of life and unexpected things that can come your way.

I decided, however though, to call it Through Isabella's Eyes.

I was so engulfed in my own pain, my childhood traumas /adult traumas, I never really thought about the impact it would have on Isabella. How she would end up growing up with traumas too. Although I didn't realise, I was doing this at the time.

I wanted to change the way that Isabella looked at the world, the view from her eyes. I didn't want it to be chaos and destruction. Sofa days and sticky floors. I wanted her to have stability, consistency, normality, and a routine that made her feel safe.

I honestly tried the hardest I could at the time. Did Belle deserve more?

Of course, she did, but when you are in addiction, it's all-consuming.

I loved her so much it hurt, but I could not stop drinking for her, making the pain unbearable.

I have mentioned rehab, but I also had to go onto some tablets called Antabuse.

These tablets are scary stuff. They break down the compounds of alcohol so you cannot drink on them, and each pill you take can stay in your system for 14 days. If you drink on them and trust me with the power of addiction, people do. I toyed back and forth with the idea, googled it, and found forums where other addicts would advise addicts how to do it effectively. How insane is that?

You can end up in hospital very, very poorly indeed. This stuff is so powerful that if you put anti-bac handwash with alcohol in on your hands, it could create a reaction, some perfumes could react from it, mouthwash, etc. It is incredible how many things have alcohol, well, ethanol, that you would never have thought of. Things like night nurse or anxiety remedies etc.

I had to be assessed to take these by a phycologist. When I first went into recovery, Christmas was just around the corner, so I felt like I needed that safety net/jump start. When we went into the world-ending scenario of lockdown etc. When everyone was using sanitiser like water. I had it engrained in my head. I couldn't use it, or I'd get ill.

I hadn't been on Antabuse for quite some time but was waiting in the ques to go into the shops. I knew someone would be standing there judging me if I didn't use it. I would get so anxious about explaining it that it would all spill out my mouth by the time I'd get to the sanitiser machine.

In reality, I could have just said I was allergic to it. I could see all the glares from the people in the queue, like I was some evil covid carrier. The same applied to the masks. They reminded me of the hospitals or some form of trauma. Remember when I said it was all fun and games at first? From very early on, I had an issue with alcohol.

By the time I was 19, I had been hospitalised from excessive drinking 4 times, including an attempted suicide.

Then as the years went on, there were more hospital stays and hospital traumas. I once had an ear infection, drank whiskey, and took too much codydramol.

I had my tummy pumped and was allergic to the Provolax they put in my system, leading to an anaphylactic shock. That was one of the scariest moments of my life. I was drowning from the inside.

My lips went over my nose. I could feel my chest filling up with fluid, I was petrified. All around me were people in masks. You would think this would be the last hospital stay, wouldn't you?

But it wasn't. It was far from it. I had to get the mental health psychiatric team out to me once because, after being so intoxicated, I could only cry and say I didn't want to live anymore. I couldn't leave my Belle, but I honestly thought she would be better off without me.

Looking back on those heart-wrenching days and how content and happy my life is now makes me feel so painfully sad.

Sad for those who have those thoughts and didn't get to find a way out or receive the help they needed.

I know a couple of people this has happened to, and it knocked me for six when I found out. To know that pain. It made me feel guilty I had found a way out of it. That's why if I can help as many people as possible, I will because I know them depths of despair.

I don't want to graphically write the levels I went to because I don't want to upset anyone who loves me, or anyone who has lost someone they love.

I honestly hit my rock bottom though, I was hanging onto a thin thread on the edge of the cliff in the darkness, that beacon, that light house that voice that said 'fight a little more' inside me was my Belle. I had completely given up, I wanted out I could not see any other way to stop this internal torment.

Then I pictured her face, her never saying 'Mommy I love you' again

Her blaming herself, her turning to addiction to cope, and somewhere deep inside me I found just enough strength to get one day sober.

I now know a peace I didn't think was possible to find, but to those who didn't. I understand, I love you, I will see you on the other side.

For you today, J

I came to light a candle today, but the giant wooden doors were closed
So, I sat on the bench nearby, hoping your spirit knows
I feel so sad for you today, but I hope you are at peace somehow
We can't understand the depths people go to, but we grieve. We pray right now
Now you don't need to believe in religion to pray for another's spirit
As long as when you pray, you mean the words that you put within it
Il light a candle at home for your sweet babies
Il light a candle for all the broken men and lost ladies
If the doors were closed on me today, maybe they have been shut on you
When you most needed solace, you knocked but just could not get in or through
It's not my business to know your reasons why
To try to understand when I cry
Because life is made up of split moments
What if living life is like every day facing your opponent
Of course, there is an aftermath for the ones left behind
But it's not for us to judge. Maybe if we did a little less of that, the world would feel kind
I sat at the bench and tried to send healing from it
Like if I was at this bench by this church, I was there and could heal others like I was a part of it
I saw daisy's all upon the church ground
So, I will loop them up and make you a crown
I'm so sorry. So many years went by with no contact. That's easy to say, though, now.
If I could, id invent the time machine, so we were on the playground playing somehow
Sleep peacefully, sometimes our biggest worry is our own mind
The bells rang ding dong ding dong chime
I went to the church today, but I couldn't get past the wooden doors

The gates of heaven are calling now, for they are open. They
are yours

Every night we sleep, I tell my daughter I love her. She tells me she loves me too, I look forward to going to sleep. I look forward to waking up. I love seeing her face when I pick her up from school. I love dropping her off at school, knowing she can tell me if she has any problems.

I told you previously, I was incredibly open and honest with my Belle about going to rehab. She wanted me to go because she wanted her happy mommy again. She wanted me to be well, knew I loved her, and I think she'd had enough.

Even my baby was withdrawing from me.

She has just turned eleven now, so she was only young at the time, so young, but she always acted mature. She was eight; she shouldn't have had to.

I call my daughter saffron sometimes from absolutely fabulous. She had those cute little glasses and definitely didn't break the rules.

She loves reading, and I never have to nag her to do her homework.

She was in a school play the other day, and I finally got to go in and see it after all this covid saga. I looked at her, up there in front of everyone, and literally, my heart just burst with pride. She is talented and loves writing and singing but is too shy to sing around anyone. At night, I took her to do our favourite thing after her play.

We go to this little chippy in Bridgnorth, and after then, I take her for Ice cream. She always gets the bubble gum flavour and mint choc chip.

On the night-time, she said to me, 'today was such a big achievement for me, Mommy' I was like, 'I know, baby, I'm so proud.'

She is in year six now and doesn't want to hold my hand.

I asked her if she wanted to join the choir, and her response was, 'ewe no, who do you think I'm trying to be, Ariana Grande.'

I cannot believe she is going into senior school next year; time does really fly.

We are moving into a new home in a couple of weeks. Some nights when we chill in doing nothing, she will be playing FIFA with Darren, and I will be typing away this book. It just feels like peace. On that note, he has been sending me some big words to put into my book, and has referred to me as Roald Dahl, which tickled me.

I read him a little segment, and he said you can't swear, and I was like, well, I wanted it to feel raw and authentic, and sometimes I swear. His chosen word was Autumnal.

He looked at me and said, 'it looks very Autumnal outside' I thought I know what's happening here.

He is trying to get me to put these words in my book. Since then, he has sent me random words.

Darren has grounded and encouraged me more than he will ever know.

When I was first with him, I would ask him if he was ok every five mins to gauge the atmosphere. I didn't need to Darren never ever creates a bad atmosphere, was just from habit.

Once I was eating prawns in my own home and apologised to him and said 'do you mind if I eat these.' Which is stupid because he likes prawns any way.

He just looked at me like 'eat whatever you want in your own home'

He tells me he is proud of me and builds me up and I do the same with him. We laugh and joke with each other and we have never ever in all the time we have known each other said anything nasty or personal to one another, we have to much respect for each other to do that.

He wouldn't ever want to deliberately upset me, and I would never want too either.

I love seeing how he is with pancake and my Belle, and that's what really matters about how my girls get treated. Consistency there has always been consistency, and that makes me feel safe. It makes Belle feel happy, too, and well, pancake is just smitten.

Belle hugs him and tells him 'I love you Darren'

Belle once said to me 'Darren completed our little family, didn't he mommy'

It's true he has and even if we split up in the future, I'd only ever want happiness for him because he has shown me what love should be.

Here is my poem.

She does not want to hold my hand.

She is growing, she is thriving, and you try to understand
That when she's at the playground, she doesn't want to hold
your hand
She is funny, she is kind she is insightful
The cuddles that she gives you when its dark outside are pure
delightful
She is learning, and she is reading on her own
So, no bedtime stories read by Mommy to set the evening tone
She talks a little now about her times on the playground
Her laugh that she gives is just the best sound
She is growing, and she is finding her own way
But you're the one she kisses when the night forms from day
You remember when those terrible twos drove you to insanity
Now you crave the days when she sat upon your knee
She is everything that is good, and that makes you want to be
A better Mother, a better person, through innocent eyes is how
she will see
She is growing, she is learning, and il try to understand
That when she's at the playground, she doesn't want to hold my
hand

Earlier in the book, I mentioned getting to do the work I love via poetry. I have set up a community interest company called Been There Done That cic.

I run workshops in schools and youth centres about addiction, mental health, domestic violence, etc. One of the best things about work is I get to take My Belle along to some of the things I do.

I sit at the front of the room and place her in the audience like a little mole in case the kids are a bit shy. She looks at me the same way I look at her.

One of my downfalls, though, is I want to try and help everyone, and I lose myself in the process and open myself up to pain. Recently someone I was doing some work with said to me that I thought I was perfect, and I looked down on people.

That couldn't be further from the truth. I doubt myself often, and some days I feel so overwhelmed that I just do not know what I am doing or feel like I'm failing. It's exhausting. The difference is now I paint the war paint on and push on through.

I don't think I am better than anyone. I hate it when people get a bit of recovery behind them and start judging people still stuck in the cycle. It is hypocritical.

What I do need to realise, though, is that's perspective. You can have a conversation and go away and think that it went well, and the other person can have a completely different view of it. Of you as a person, or think you may have an agenda etc, lots of these things again come from fear.

You try to be nice, but because they have been hurt so bad in the past, they think there is an agenda. That's a shame; really, everyone's trauma is different.

It may come across that way.

I would hate to be patronising or seem self-absorbed. Another thing I know is if someone is talking about something they are going through. I know that pain and can empathise. I will relate or reference it to something as if to say I know how you feel. I understand now that it may seem like I am trying to take the limelight or lessen their pain and make it about me. I really don't mean to.

I need to learn to listen more, and not be so quick to open my mouth. But I find that difficult because I just want to give solutions, but sometimes people just need an open ear, and it's not about me.

Like I said, though, in recovery terms, I am still a baby and learning.

I make mistakes. I am not too happy with my weight, but I eat emotionally.

Every time I plan to go to the gym. I do it intensely for 3 days, then nothing.

If I do not see results after 3 days, I am fuming. I know the gym makes me feel better, but I just haven't seemed to be able to find the time. However, nothing stops me from prancing around the flat with my weights.

Why not do something you know makes you feel better?

Because it's inconvenient, I'd rather watch Netflix, slob, eat, and then feel shit about myself.

'No, Beth, type up your book, do your exercises, stop buying trainers and other useless shit off the internet, and stop trying to hold yourself back like a bungee rope.'

Conflictions of the Mind

The conflictions of the mind.
Internal conflictions of a recovering mind
Dents in the armour it's always trying to find
If it can't grow from your fear, it goes for your dreams
Muddles your whole head up, so nothing's as it seems
Won't let you observe positive outcomes. Don't you dare feel
proud
Because that's when all the insecurities bang drums and scream
really loud
You overcome the fear and learn to sit in all the pain
But it was leering in the shadows, as predictable as summers
rain
It whispers in your ear when you are learning to drive
It holds you back like bungee ropes. How dare you try to thrive
It replays conversations and says, 'oh, you should not have said
that.'
Until you don't want to communicate with other humans, happy
hiding in the flat
It tries to find an opening to drip poison into your ear
It knows you won't reach for the bottle, so it turns your dreams
into pure fear
Who exactly is it that you are trying to be
Get back into your box, for dreams are not for me
Yet I choose to keep on pushing through on auto-pilot mode
Every now and then, though, my mind just cannot take the load
It's not that I would reach for those bottles on the top shelf
I just have days when I really should be kinder to myself.
Who the fuck cares for poetry? You're driving really shit
All it takes is a drop of the mic, or a swerve to the curb for a hit
So don't you think it would be better here sitting in this flat
You can't do what you think you can do. ACTUALLY, I CAN,
AND THAT'S A FACT
'You should be a better Mother. You should work harder, clean
harder, and drive better
Laa dee dar poetry, I mean, there's not much power within a
letter

113

'Actually, there is, but you don't like it when I write it down. It releases it from my head.'
'You would rather I sit and wallow with ice cream on my top inside my bed.'
But I won't, 'I am far much more than you tried to make me
You might not like the movements I do now daily
This is because every step I take is a step forward, even with you screaming in my head
So, although I know I'm fighting you, this addiction is far from dead

Eyes

Eyes, they say, are portals to the soul and open doors of
reflection
Glazed over in fear, waterfalls in sadness, stone cold for
protection
They say a lot about a person. I don't mean the colour or the
size
I mean, you can see when someone's hurting or kindness in
one's eyes
When someone is in a bad place, it's like the light behind them
fades
They don't glimmer like the moonlight does when it shines
upon the waves
But when eyes are happy, they smile and glisten. They sparkle
Empty eyes can one day shine again and be beautiful
It's just the darkness sometimes can cloud them with sorrow
I wish you could see you how I see you, wish my eyes you
could borrow
So, you can see just how beautiful you are even when your
lights are low
I wish I could turn back on the lights, but that's something only
you can do though
Eyes give away so much. I can tell by someone's eyes if they
are trapped in addiction
They are red like roses, but it's like they are lost in a garden,
and no one's picked them
They dance in whirlpools when lost in liquid I never even
recognised
That the light was fading behind my own eyes
Mine sparkle again, and yours can do too
If you just let out those tears you hold in, you
Squeeze out the resentment that makes them scowl and bitter
Throw them away like last year's litter
They say eyes are the portal of the soul. They open doors of
reflection
But if you blink too quick, you may forget them
The eyes you have upon your head
Could glow in happiness does not glaze in Red

115

Chapter Nine

The Move

So, I've just moved into a new home, it is beautiful; it's more rural, at the end of the road there's a wooden shack, the bus stop. At the back of my house is a massive field which you can look at when washing up. I thought about getting a dishwasher but found something therapeutic in looking out the window and washing up. I have been in my home for a week today, and it's all coming together nicely.

(Much longer, you know the drill)

This time last week, I was a broken woman, the disorder of boxes everywhere raised my anxiety through the roof. It reminded me of a time when my life was pure chaos. My previous flat was two flights upstairs with no lift. So, we had to move boxes and boxes of stuff up and down the stairs, and it was a lot.

I chucked about 15 bags of rubbish away that I found in the draws and cupboards and just general shit we found along the way or clothes I promised myself I would wear again but never have.

I had started my new tenancy on my house and had to be out of my old flat, but as part of the conditions, I had to rip up all the carpets, etc.

No matter how many times I went up and down the stairs, more bags seemed to appear, and I just wanted to cry.

I did not know why I felt this way, because I knew I was going on to more remarkable and better things, and it was something I had wanted for so long.

Moving, in general, triggers a lot of feelings for anyone, and for me, it was every other time I moved. It was because I had been running away from something but this time, I was moving on to better things.

The last time I lived in a house, it was a home where I was very unwell, and there was an aspect of fear, could I handle a whole house again?

I was trying to work in the daytime and then pack everything up during the night, and I was exhausted. Although I knew I was packing because I was leaving in a few days, the boxes, and the disorganisation of everything made me feel mentally unwell and overwhelmed.

This week, however, I feel a million miles away from the person I was last week.

I just wanted everything new, so I got a lot of it on finance, but I pay those bills off now.

I have not got cash to splash about, but my previous things were uncomfortable, and I wanted to make this home a home that lasts with things that last.

I spoke to Belle's school when we were moving and explained to them that I felt it would be good for Belle to be part of the moving process, primarily due to the reasons why we have moved before. Fair play to them.

They authorised Belle a day off school. The school Belle goes to now is lovely. Anyway, after I signed for the keys etc, my anxiety was getting me to the point I could not breathe. I thought I needed to take time away from this situation and find peace.

So, we went exploring and came across this place called Daniels Mill, a big old-fashioned mill house with a café, so we stopped off for some food. It started to rain, and there wasn't any room inside, so she said we could sit under a big umbrella thing and eat until a seat became available.

There was something quite calming about the rain. We ordered some food, and then after a short while, the lady offered us inside. She had this aura that reminded me of my Nanny Win. She was kind, and her voice was soft and sweet. Belle had a pot of tea in a China tea set, and I had a cappuccino with cinnamon on the top.

Fairy lights wrapped around the wood fixtures and a log fire burned inside. This was a little bit of heaven and what I needed during all the chaos. The food tasted beautiful, and I just felt a feeling of calm come over me.

The point is that on any other day, I may not have appreciated all the little finer details in this café or the feeling it gave me. I may not have looked at the little log burner and smiled quite as much if it had been any other day. Sometimes the most unexpected, beautiful things can happen in the middle of storms.

We had never been to this side of Bridgnorth before, and it is so rural it has no paths. We didn't want to keep walking down the side of the roads on the little grass banks because it put us on edge, so we asked the lovely lady if she knew another way.

She directed us a way that was through like a mini forest with a stream and footpaths that had got all sludgy in the rain. Belle was slightly scared, so she wanted to hold my hand. That was the first time in forever she wanted to hold my hand, and it felt so lovely.

We made our way back and eventually got back to the old flat to spend our last night there before the big move. We watched a film together and said bye to the old home we were leaving. Still full of love, but we had just outgrown it and were on to better things.

At one point on Saturday, when I was moving, I managed to trip over a bin bag and wee myself a little bit, which was fun, much to my brother Hen's amusement. He didn't know about the wee at that point. He saw me trapped on the floor and started launching more bin bags at me.

(Hen's a good lad. His one of my best friends, and we can talk to each other about anything, we rip the piss out of each other, and he does not sugar-coat things, but I am fortunate to have him, not as lucky as he is to have me obviously but non the less even though he is Propper muppet, I love him a lot.)

I can laugh about that now because I'm not in that situation. I even went to the Doctor to get some diazepam for my anxiety. She gave me five 2mg ones to use in extreme emergencies. I guess it's the addict's background, aha. I went there to be proactive and say, 'Look, I feel overwhelmed, but I don't in any way, shape, or form want to drink.'

Anyhow, I took one and had to get Belle from school. The only thing it managed to relax was my bloody bowels, so on the way walking back, I had to run into this pub, much to my absolute dismay, and go to the loo. Belle kept going, 'hurry up, Mommy,' making me even more embarrassed. When I left, the barmaid looked at me like I know what you have just done. I thought, 'for fuck's sake, thanks for that, Belle.'

118

I Had to go back to the flat and still move out lodes of other stuff.

So, moving is stressful, especially when you piss and nearly shit yourself, but I can look back and laugh.

I can also laugh and how ridiculous my mindset was back in addiction.

(I vacuumed water up once. I told myself one more drink would sober me up. I thought if I wore bright red lipstick and oversized faux fur coats, no one would know I was pissed. No, I just looked like pat butcher after a night on the sambucas at the Vic.)

I also know if I continue to learn and work on myself, in a few years, I'll look back at who I am today and be like, she needed to get a grip.

It is also easy to lose gratitude for all the things you are blessed with when you feel overwhelmed, insecure, or out of your depth.

This week I am wrapped in gratitude, joy, and peace, and it really is amazing how your mindset can change when you have a full belly and a good night's sleep.

My baby has had a bike but has never been interested in learning to ride it. She has always preferred her scooter.

When we were in the flat, getting the bike down all the flights of stairs was a nightmare.

Well, I looked out my window. Belle had her little helmet on, and she had taught herself to ride it. She taught herself to swim too.

She never fails to amaze me or make me feel proud.

I have now been in my new home for four months. Yes, we have even slipped into 2023. My best friend stayed last night. My best friend has been my best friend since I was fourteen. There were three of us growing up Manda, Kate, and I. Manda has seen all the different versions of me, the breakups, the hairstyles, the clothes, etc.

We have been there for each other through everything. She was there for me when my Nan died, and I have also been there for her when her grandparents died. She was there at the Birth of Isabella, and she is the mother of the girl Amelia I mentioned earlier, the eighteenth Birthday I attended.

It was so lovely to show her my new home. We got a pie from the local butcher's proper homemade pie and decided to watch twilight re-live our youth a bit. It is strange when you watch something like that again after years.

We kind of dissected all the dramatic acting, and we ripped the piss a bit. It was lovely to show her my home, my happiness, and all my new lotions and potions. I used to use her makeup when we were younger, which drove her bloody mad, but she has all the best stuff, and I'd always feel a million dollars when I used it. So, seeing I finally have my own, aha was nice for her.

We had a right laugh going down memory lane, and I asked her if it would be ok to read her a few chapters of the book. She couldn't really say no. To be fair would have been a bit harsh like. She loved it, though, how honest, and authentic it was, so it kind of gave me the push to get back to it and hit that deadline I had set myself for my thirty-fifth Birthday.

I said about us going for a walk in the morning, so I could show her all the fields at the back. I gave her my bed, and I slept downstairs. We have shared the bed hundreds of times over the years, but I like my own space now.

Plus, I snore and do not want to wake her up. Darren has referred to it as a bore in the bed, so I didn't want to subject her to that.

I went to the doctor about it this week, and they changed some of my tablets. They are going to put me in for some tests.

It may be allergy-related, so they gave me some drowsy antihistamines, which are suitable for stopping the ticking head. I take nytol sometimes, but it doesn't half give you vivid dreams.

In the last couple of years, on Manda's Birthday, she has gone out with our other friends for a drink, but in the daytime, we book into a lovely spa. It's an alternative that is nice and good for both of us to refresh and unwind.

It was important to distance myself from some of my past friends that were more drinking buddies, but our friendship is far deeper than that. I have a few close friends I have grown up with that have supported me too. I guess it's just good sometimes to keep groups of friends separate.

That's where I have made mistakes before.

We are looking into booking a wellness retreat with other ladies we know doing yoga Reiki etc.

I've never cleared my mind enough to meditate, but it would be good to keep trying.

(Although Darren told me this top tip about using green tea bags under my eyes to relax, so I was lying on my living room floor with tea bags on my eyes listening to healing sound bowls trying too zen out.

I caught a glimpse of pancake looking at me like 'what the fuck is this lunatic doing now,' then she started licking the bloody tea juice off my face.

I looked at her bout ten mins later though, she had got well into the sound bowls was looking very chilled indeed, may have been the chamomile in my tea bag aha.)

We have been friends so long we know each other inside out; she would know if I was lying or sad. We can be honest with each other, even if we don't necessarily want to hear what is said.

True friendship is not telling your friend what they want to hear for an easy life. It's being honest and looking out for their best intentions. So, when I read her the book, she replied how much she loved it, it meant so much because I don't think she would ever set me up to fail if it sounded like utter drivel and garbage. She would tell me. However, if it does and you all hate this book, it's all Amanda's fault.

Little Moments

We chase little moments of peace
A hot bath, on cold days, or a family feast
Little moments of serenity
When all the other moments can feel, well, empty
We run around doing the mundane
Because we must, although chores are a pain
So, we chase little moments of peace
A fancy hot coffee, seconds of silence, or a family feast
We change our priorities
We were all about friends, now it's back to days with our
families
We love our friends. They are shaping their own lives
Whether that be single and sassy or resolute housewives
We can feel like we are not entirely on par with others
Don't have sticker charts and organic things like some mothers
But what are we comparing ourselves to?
If I'm comparing myself to my old self, then I've got news for
you
You are walking on coals, and you are stepping on fire
When the voices said that you couldn't well, they were a liar
You have Down days; give yourself a break and stop being so
hard on yourself all the time
Life gave you lemons, but you prefer limes
Zesty, just like the fruitfulness of the new world you creating
So, stop debating
In this tornado, this whirlwind, life like a storm
We die; we don't always live from the day we are born
We are not immortal, yet we live like we are and moan about
the mundane
We create our own chores, although we know it's a pain
A walk all alone with nature or a family feast
They are our blessings, those little moments of peace

We have been moved in two weeks today, cough six months, and wow, this place feels like our little part of heaven. Just shows what a difference your environment can make to your mental health.

At the back of the house are fields that go on forever. Yesterday I took a walk over them. The countryside air was so beautiful, just me and my music, and I forgot how much I needed to walk and exercise for my mental health. It blows away the cobwebs from my mind and helps me process things without feeling overwhelmed.

I ran out of fags yesterday, but that was a blessing because, lately, my chest has been feeling heavy. I have gone from smoking a few fags a day to over ten, that might not sound that much. But financially it really is, and also, I can feel it on my chest and see it in the lines under my eyes and the colour of my teeth.

What is the point in spending all this money on face cream and toothpaste if I smoke and damage myself from the inside?

I always thought I'd do it when I was ready, so I will try to go onto the vape and take it from there.

I walked over the fields today to try suppressing my addictive mind craving, and it worked. The fresh air, the views, the peace, and the weather was excellent for this time of year.

I just threw some clothes on and never put a bra on.

I bumped into this couple walking their dog and started a quick conversation, then realised I never had a bra on and blurted it out to them. Sometimes I can be so socially awkward.

I thought after I bet that woman thought why she is telling my fella she hasn't got a bra on. I went to start worrying about it, but instead, I just giggled to myself and said, 'oh well, floppy tits, let's keep walking.'

I have been feeling great for the last two weeks. That may be down to my environment, my antidepressants going up 10mg, or some of the superb supplements I have been trying lately.

While walking earlier, I thought it's time to strip things back a bit and take the pressure off myself. Do some work to finish this book finally.

In fairness, in a way, it's good I never did because I can add things in now, and it has been great to see how things have changed over time, like an extensive wordy diary.

It's been my little project from a scrapbook to a laptop, to making my dream as a child of being a writer a reality.

I've always loved writing; I love how you can read a book and get transported into its pages. I wanted to take you all on a truthful journey with me that would hopefully help some of you.

I wanted to do it for that broken version of myself and be like. 'Hey, you, if it wasn't for your pain, I wouldn't have had this tale to tell; it was your path all along, younger nutjob self. I don't hate you anymore. Sorry I wasn't kinder to you; this book is my gift. I'm hugging you with its words and undoing all those nasty things you told yourself you were or let others tell you, you are not those things. You are kind, love deeply, and want to be part of the change process. You were just a little lost; it was all just a bit too much; it was all you knew; your dark days led me to these ones. Thank you for carrying the load; I'll take it from here; Belle's happy; you met someone who loves you, who is kind. Your Family are proud; the world is much nicer now'

Chapter Ten

Horrible Hormones

So, I have just come back to this chapter after a couple of weeks. I decided it was time to come off my pill for a while, the hormonal one. I am on one that stops you from getting a period altogether, and I just feel like I need a break from it. Not having that release doesn't feel right; I knew it would make me feel strange, and it has. I have had such a lack of energy that it felt like a period brewing. Still, it's just refusing to come out, which is even more frustrating because I feel like I have all the other symptoms.

I figured I would hit a low peak before they returned to normal.

I have been doing work with my friend Emily, who works at Newman university. We went there as she was doing a presentation, and she pulled me in as a guest speaker.

After the presentation, the groups were asked if they would create a CIC and what they would make it on. I was helping one group, and because it was fresh in my mind, I brought up hormones and how they are underestimated but can affect many aspects of your life.

The University is in Birmingham, so many different cultures go there, it was so interesting listening to some of the girls and how they are made to feel dirty when they are on their period.

In some cultures, women are not allowed in the kitchen or house. It is frowned upon and would bring disgrace to the family if they were to go on a form of contraception to help with their menstrual flow.

It really got me thinking about lots of things. How before I am due on my period, I get a wave of depression and anxiety during that point; statistically, ladies have been known to relapse due to periods and what it would be like if you had an assignment due in the alleviated levels of anxiety.

We have groups like AA, NA, etc. We came up with an idea of a forum where women could freely talk about the effects of their period, from flow to PMT, cravings, and cultural aspects, and whereby they could help each other without judgment.

When I first had my period, I was a teenager living with my dad, so that's awkward, and I think some, not all, men think PMT is something we have made up so we can just act like a bitch for a week.

During those times, though, we lose ourselves, doubt ourselves, and feel indecisive, dirty, bloated, and fat, so it's not something we enjoy.

If you had others you could talk to about it, it may help.

We are in 2023 and periods are still a taboo subject, it is crazy when you think about it but in all honesty, the world seems a bit crazy at the moment. I'll get onto the so-called cost of living crisis in a while.

This book is not just designed for females, though. Our conversation got onto the pressures of the male image and how young men abuse testosterone without realising the damage it will do them in later life. The mood swings, the low feelings, etc.

We just do not talk to each other enough about these things. If we explained how we were feeling and why we think we may feel that way more often, there would be fewer misunderstandings.

We take things out on our nearest and dearest, and we keep our partners out of the loop sometimes because we want to appear safe and strong.

There is no harm in explaining 'I am feeling low in mood because of PMT, or a bad day or, you don't really know why your spirits dropped, but please bear with me. It truly is not you. So sorry I may have overreacted. It's just I'm feeling a bit sensitive right now.'

Wow seems a lot easier to just be a bitch, doesn't it? and kick off about the bins not going out or the toilet seat being up.

In the long run, though, it is not because you're suddenly in a blazing row about trivial things that turn into the big things where you both get hurt. Hurt each other's feelings, and you weren't even that arsed, he pissed on the seat, really. Not to the point of a screaming match etc. So, it may be easier overall just talking.

Our minds do overtime when we have hormonal imbalances, and we question everything so nip it in the bud before it spirals.

Or create a forum but just make sure you don't all hype yourselves up to kick ass because they can make us a tad irrational, too, (just a tiny bit though.)

I wonder why we crave chocolate so much when we are due on, like an addict to heroin. I thought it was just menstrual craving. We feel like a vacuum has sucked all our energy, we feel exhausted, and everyday things feel like a long-winded chore. We need a pick-me-up, I suppose, but then I googled it to see what it said, because it is not just one or two people who crave it. It's a well-known thing, worldwide so I thought there must be some scientific reason.

So here it is.

(You need quick energy. Hormonal fluctuations during the menstrual cycle led to fatigue, especially pre-period. If you crave chocolate during this time, your body may be crying out for more energy, or you may have low blood sugar. Chocolate contains a small number of stimulants like caffeine and theobromine.

One of the symptoms of PMS is increased food cravings and overeating. People with PMS crave different foods, including chocolate, and they tend to eat more than usual. There is no specific reason for craving chocolate, but we know that during the luteal phase, we crave more carbs, sweets, and fats.)

I found this information while googling, I doubt have a clue what luteal means aha.

Since I have been in recovery, I have learned a lot about the moon and mercury retrograde and other things that can affect our feelings and behaviours. This may be why my dad says I should have a crystal ball and a robe, but I know he knows some of it's true.

Well, I do little rituals on a full moon, not like sacrificing a goat or anything, just setting out intentions, burning things that hold me back, not items or people. (Just to clarify) I write them down. I don't start burning exes or my year 5 music teacher who never let me join the choir because she didn't like my big brother, battle axe bitch. (Clearly not quite over that,) charging my crystals, grounding etc.

One of the things it says to do is drink cocoa, so I got googling that too.

(Building a personal moon ritual with cacao. As described above, setting our intentions on the new moon can be powerful.

And when we add the heart-opening plant medicine that is ceremonial-grade cacao and truly tune in to our heart's desires, the effects get amplified, and we can literally create miracles. The theobromine in cacao increases blood flow to the heart, which has the effect of 'opening it up so we can better hear its guidance, wisdom, and the messages found within)

Again google.

In a way, when we are on our period, we are so full of rage we sometimes say the things that really bother us, like a short window of time to express how we feel. Is it all connected in some way?

Maybe, for years people went by the cycle of the moon. Our periods are a cycle. Both involve chocolate. I mean, this book is not about me dissecting all that, and I do not want to go too far off track, but if you would like to open your mind a bit more and you have some time on your hands could be something you could look into, perhaps.

I also want to let you know I have tried a CBD-infused drink which felt terrific and chilled me out. Before I knew it, in one week, I had spent sixty pounds on those said drinks, so keep an eye on these things and ensure you're not chasing highs.

I like the drink but not that much. That's alcoholic kind of cash on drinks, and we have moved on from that foolishness.

So, let's not get into that because before we know it, we will be drinking 25 cans of it a day, chasing that first moment of calm, wondering where all our money has gone, and we are not in times where we can do that at the moment.

At Christmas time, I went away to Tenerife with my family. It was my first holiday since being in recovery abroad due to lockdowns, and I was excited but nervous.

I hadn't in my whole adult life done the airport sober. I remember it being about three am before, and some woman was sitting there drinking green tea, and I thought she was the scum of the earth. Who drinks green tea at the airport? Let's start this party as you start your holiday in Wetherspoons and pay about eight pounds for a shot of vodka on the plane.

I needed some sun, though; Belle needed some sun, and while I sat around the pool reading the first few chapters, I wrote, watching Belle splash about it felt like heaven.

A bar opposite our hotel, though, played music absolutely blasting till 2am every night. I moved away from directly opposite all the way up the street and could still hear it.

I know in my logical mind people are on holiday. They are just having fun, and I never want to begrudge any of them. Still, it was an inconvenience that overshadowed things because I am a grouchy bitch if I don't have enough sleep, I was keeping myself safe by going out for an evening meal and returning before the party-goers descended. So, it's like welcoming the party to your living room almost. It was raging me far more than usual inconveniences do.

I wanted to scream at the top of my lungs 'shut the fuck up, who gives a fuck about sweet fucking Caroline, and if one more person sings build me up butter cup, I'm going to seriously smash heads in,' I contemplated going over there and smashing the place up a few times as I tossed and turned. I never because remember, I'm all peaceful, enlightened, and all that jazz now. (Fucking Holiday loving, karaoke singing bell ends)

Then one night, I got that pain I hadn't had for a while because I'd been on the pill that stopped them, and oh god, it hurt like a bitch. It explained the rage though, just a bit. It was my lovely jubbly period. It had waited till I was away to say 'hi' because we all love feeling even more bloated on holiday.

Darren, or Jarren as my nephew calls him aha, was in England because he still had work, and one night my head attacked me about him. 'Why would he want to be with you?'

'I bet he hates you because you're away. He's probably going to have gotten married to someone else in the week you're away.'

'They probably live in your house and have adopted pancake, and you will just have to live in the shed' (I hate that bitch. Who is she? where is she? I'll fight her)'

That kind of shit, aha.

(don't act like you don't do it because we all go nuts during the dreaded time)

I kind of knew it was just my head playing tricks. I just texted him the next day a simple 'hi babe, are you ok' and yea everything was absolutely fine. Imagine if I'd fuelled all that hormonal imagination with booze. I probably would have been coming home to no partner because he would have thought I was insane.

Because I am sober now, I can identify these tricks of the mind. I managed to get some sleeping tablets from a chemist, and I found a place that sold sage, so I sagged all those negative thoughts away.

I loved that holiday with my family in the sun, but I was excited to come home to my beautiful home for the first time. I missed my dog and Darren and my bed. Nothing better than your own bed.

Chapter Eleven

The Good Stuff

Remember I mentioned that I take some supplements. I thought I would share some with you. You can do your own research and find out what best suits you, but I'm going to make a short list of them and a summary of their benefits.

Anyhow here is a list of goodies that may help you.

Sea Moss Gel

Builds a strong immune system, and a strong immune system is linked to a healthy stomach. Sea moss is also rich in iron and antioxidants, both of which support a healthy immune system.

There are both beneficial and dangerous bacteria in your digestive system. Balancing out those bacteria is crucial to your wellness because gut health is linked to overall health. Sea moss and other algae are excellent sources of living bacteria and fibre.

One of the components of a healthy thyroid is iodine, but since your body cannot produce iodine on its own, you must obtain it through nutrition.

Seaweed is a superfood. It contains more fibre than most vegetables, which is advantageous because fibre provides a variety of health benefits for the body. It can help you better manage your blood sugar, lower cholesterol, and minimize your risk of developing long-term conditions like diabetes and heart disease.

Additionally, seaweed has calcium which aids in protecting against brittle bones, which helps to protect against osteoporosis.

It also protects against cancer due to the calcium, iodine, and sodium alginate found in seaweed.

For reference, this information was found on https://somethingbettertoday.com/

(Oh, look at me referencing like a professional)

Black Seed Oil
Packed With Antioxidants
May Lower Cholesterol
Could Have Cancer-Fighting Properties
It can Help Kill off Bacteria
May Alleviate Inflammation
Could Help Protect the Liver
Can Aid in Blood Sugar Regulation
It may Prevent Stomach Ulcers

Chlorophyll
- increased energy
- hormonal balance
- arthritis and fibromyalgia relief
- weight loss

Chlorophyll has shown potential as a cancer treatment in some tests conducted on animals:
- A 2015 review concluded that chlorophyllin might help prevent and slow cancer growth.
- A study Trusted from 2005 found that natural chlorophyll reduced the risk of colon cancer in rats. The rats ate a diet high in red meat and low in green vegetables, which has associations with an increased risk of colon cancer. However, the authors did not see the same results for chlorophyllin.
- A 2016 study found that chlorophyllin helped slow the progression of lung cancer in mice. The researchers administered chlorophyllin to the mice in microscopic capsules known as nanocapsules.

Topical chlorophyll may work as an anti-aging remedy. A study by Trusted found that applying a gel containing chlorophyllin to the skin reduced signs of photoaging, which is aging, that results from sun exposure. The study used skin samples from four healthy women and lasted for 12 days.

The results of the study showed that skin treated with chlorophyllin improved in a similar way to skin treated with tretinoin, which is a prescription skin cream that has been proven to help with skin aging. The authors suggest that using a combination of chlorophyllin and tretinoin could be an effective treatment for reversing the signs of photoaged skin.

For reference purposes, this information was found on www.medicalnewstoday.com

Turmeric
Health Benefits of Turmeric
1. Depression
2. Type 2 Diabetes
3. Viral Infections
4. Premenstrual Syndrome
5. High Cholesterol
6. Alzheimer's Disease
7. Arthritis
8. Cancer
9. irritable bowel syndrome
10. Headaches
11. Acne

Manuka Honey
1. Aid Wound Healing
2. Promote Oral Health
3. Soothe a Sore Throat
4. Help Prevent Gastric Ulcers
5. Improve Digestive Symptoms
6. May Treat Symptoms of Cystic Fibrosis
7. Treat Acne

Ashwagandha
1. Is an ancient medicinal herb
2. Can reduce blood sugar levels
3. Might have anticancer properties
4. Can reduce cortisol levels
5. May help reduce stress and anxiety

Sage
1. High in Several Nutrients
2. Loaded with Antioxidants
3. May Support Oral Health

4. May Ease Menopause Symptoms
5. May Reduce Blood Sugar Levels
6. May Support Memory and Brain Health
7. May Lower "Bad" LDL Cholesterol
8. May Protect Against Certain Cancers
9. May alleviate diarrhoea
Also lighting sage can give you a calming effect.

Ginkgo Balaba
1. Holds Powerful Antioxidants
2. Can Help Fight Inflammation
3. Improves Circulation and Heart Health
4. Reduces Symptoms of Psychiatric Disorders and Dementia
5. Improves Brain Function and Wellbeing
6. Can Reduce Anxiety
7. Can Treat Depression
8. Can Support Vision and Eye Health

Lions Mane Mushroom
The lion's mane mushroom is a large fungus with a distinctive shaggy appearance and a long history in Chinese traditional medicine. It's known for its nootropic ability to focus your mind and keep your brain alert. It is also an adaptogen and can restore a healthy balance to your body's vital systems.

Chaga Mushroom
Cell health includes promoting healthy skin, giving you a natural energy boost, and boosting your immune system as it has exceptionally high levels of antioxidants. Packed full of Magnesium, Zinc, Potassium, and Vitamin D. It's also a great source of Melanin.

Shiitake Mushroom
Brilliant for Heart Health, Shiitake is packed full of eritadenine, a compound known to reduce cholesterol levels in the blood. Also containing beta-glucans means it can help reduce inflammation and helps stop your body from absorbing cholesterol.

Royal Sun Mushroom
Liver Function and Natural Immune Response. It's the best friend for autoimmune disorders and allergies, and thanks to it being rich in lipids and Vitamin B it can help boost liver function.

Reishi Mushroom
The mushroom of vitality. Reishi can enhance your immune system, reduce stress, and improve your sleep.

Turkey Tail Mushroom
The Immunity Mushroom. Known to have benefits on the liver and gut bacteria, this mushroom is a prebiotic and immune system booster in one.

Maitake Mushroom
Also known as Hen-of-the-Wood, Maitake is great for your metabolism. Beta glucan helps reduce cholesterol, improve artery function, and improve overall cardiovascular health.

For reference (here I go again)

All this information was found on google. I researched each item, got fixated, and now have cupboards of vitamins instead of vodka.

I'm guessing by now you get the drift and see the pattern. 'Please take my depression away, oh mighty supplements, and make my skin nice while you are there.'

Remember when I talked about Cross addiction? If I see a crystal shop, I am literally like a magpie.

I simply do not seem to have the ability to save. It's like money burns a hole in my pocket. You get the same feelings but not as intense as active addiction. High, high, high when you have got money, spending money, going home using the things you spent the money on.

Low, low, low when you spend your money, you see you have ten of the same things, but in different colours and an even bigger low when you buy something fucking stupid off the internet again, like the time I brought myself teeth from Instagram and looked like the Jim Carey from as the fucking mask.

Or when I ordered some mushroom stalls for an idea, I randomly had pop in my head that I fixated on until I brought them. I decided I was going to turn my garden into a fairy kingdom. When they came off eBay around 2 weeks later, they were the size of bloody skittles. You may have mistaken them for funky-looking Ecstasy tablets, not big garden magical mushrooms I just had to get for my garden.

I suddenly decided that at 10 pm, I was going to create a fairy wonderland. It is winter; I would start collecting the stuff before spring. I might as well have brought marbles because I've lost a few over the years.

Will I get some form of ADHD, Bi-Polar or any other diagnosis anytime soon? I doubt it. You could have a heart attack there, and then the Doctor's receptionist would still ask you what your problem was so she could refuse an appointment.

You call dead on the dot to get in queue lines open at 8.30, and you call at 8.30. There are forty-five people in the queue in front of you. You walk down there the queue is out the door. A referral process will take a while. Let's put it on the to-do list ay.

(Actually, I got into the Doctor's surgery, and I am awaiting a diagnosis) I also have dyslexia; it's a bit strange that I have got this far down the book without mentioning that but thank God for finding Grammarly. Being able to pick up on the many errors my dyslexic mind makes.

These are little hurdles, though, the unique quirks that make me who I am. If you look at it further, actually dyslexic people arc vcry crcative, and people with ADHD can think outside of the box, so I do not see these as setbacks at all. That's the problem sometimes people see these things as unfavourable but don't see the beauty in them. Also, who wants to be textbook normal anyway?

Not me! I've ordered myself a crystal crown to wear in the bath, because well I just fucking want to, if people knew would they think I was weird. Yes, do I care anymore, Ermm No, (bet they wish they had a crystal crown for the bath, and they could pretend they was a mermaid too, but they are too busy caring about what every other fucker thinks.)

The likely hood is no matter how many times I go through this book, there will be errors somewhere. I am not professing to be an intellect. I got kicked out of school for my behaviour just before my GCSEs. I've got an Education along the way but nothing like a degree. So, if you haven't got lodes of letters after your name either, you could do something like this too. The same applies if you want to go get some. You can achieve your dreams. I'm achieving mine by doing this.

I went to see a holistic therapist in Bridgnorth last week called Angie. I liked her instantly I could tell she was a good person. She worked wonders on me realigned my back and I went out of there feeling so much better. I want to try acupuncture and cupping and lots of other things. I have angel reiki healing from a lady named bobbie who is fab too. Would I ever of tried these things in active addiction no I would of spent money on intoxicating myself not bettering myself. my beautiful, kind soul friend Jo, I work with who is an art teacher, we went for some sound healing together and wow did it work.

All of the lovely jubbly things I listed can be found online, but I used to like to go up to Birmingham Bullring and get fresh stuff from the markets.

Some of the little places you find up there are like Aladdin's cave of goodies. The Oasis market is like hippie central lodes of quirky little shops promoting zen and tranquillity. We spend so long behind a computer screen that we can forget what reality is. I don't mean normal town centre shopping I mean the little market stalls and quirky shops with lovely petty things in them.

I have a picture on my wall that says a face without freckles is like a night without stars. I love it. I love all that kind of stuff. It might not be to everyone's taste, but I wrote a couple of poems about the rawness of Birmingham. I do not want to move back, but I can still appreciate those places.

So here are a couple of poems I wrote.

I am a Bench in Birmingham

I am a bench in Birmingham placed in pigeon park
I see the sights of odd delights in this city when it's dark
Some people have even used my steel at night, staying on it like
a bed
Cannot imagine my metal frame would be comfy for your head
I see people all kinds of people on a daily basis
I'm in the centre of most of it all, a stone's throw from oasis
I have seen the different fashion trends the goths, the Emos and
the chavs
I have seen people loved up in town and buggy bashings to
baby dads
I am kind of in the middle here. As I said, oasis just a stone's
throw
Then you have all the posho bars placed upon Colmore row
I see people hurriedly running to snow hill in suits
Looking frustrated by their daily commutes
Many a person has sat and eaten a pound baguette
I have been piddled on by a passer-by's pet
I am a bench in Birmingham. They painted my iron blue
If you need to rest for a while, I'll take the weight off you
For I have seen many things over the many years
But I'll take the rust upon my skin to hold you through your
tears
I may just seem like an object, just a simple bench to you
But I have seen so many things, and I have a tale or two

Oasis Market

City centres where the smell of weed overpowers the smell of
Joop
And traffic gets stuck on islands circling around in a loop
Gregg's sausage rolls replace dummies
It's buy1 get one free on CBD gummies
From the man at the market that's probably selling you fruit
pastels
Homeless people turn cardboard into their Fort castles
There just seems to be
More visible poverty
But city centres are the best places to people watch
Watching children walking behind parents avoiding the cracks
and playing hopscotch
Fake trainers and Ganga leaf hats
Bob Marley t-shirts to go with that
Que in MacDonald's is not quite so fast food
They have run out of cheese sticks puts you in a mood
People on laptops
In coffee shops
Buskers singing their hearts out for people to throw them
pennies
And the look of despair gives you heartburn. You need Rene's
Because your heart hurts for the homeless
So, you offer him a KFC he goes for the option boneless
I think that is what people can be
No backbone when it comes to conspiracy
These people are not people. They are statistics
If you can buy them a coffee, accompany it with some biscuits
Different food, different clothes, different religions
That either set people free or put them in a prayer books prison
Depends on what you do in the name of it
But that's nothing new wars were fought for it
City centres where you see fake Uggs and juicy couture
Baccy numbs are being taken from bins galore
But if you are walking through one take a second or so
Treat people like humans as you go

Chelmsley Wooder

A Chelmsley Wooder
Typically labelled as a no gooder
You talk to your neighbour, but you do not really trust one
another
Men tend to like to use the word Baby Mother
They're trying to do it up with things like that new ASDA
Bright house warriors with there with a 50-inch Plasma
And when your dole has been stopped well, that is just a
disaster
Shut the door on your high-rise, and well it is just happily ever
after
Born and bred in Yardley
Is it any better there, nah, hardly?
Crazy days as a youth well, they've just dam scared me
The new inns local, just like a youth party
We all do things of which we deny
We all got our fingers in more than one pie
And yes, we beg, steal and borrow just to get by
I have pulled a trick or two not going to lie
People seem contented in just struggling along
You get high from the corner shop, knocked out by the pong
Of the chronic that has been sucked through a 14-year-old's
bong
The dress code is simply not particularly hard to get wrong
You are just sick to death of topping up that metre
Got to get yourself a tipple and end up getting a vodka litre
The men aren't exactly prime meat or a keeper
He cannot take u for a meal that is half his job seekers

THE STRANGERS IN OUR STORY

Strangers play a significant role in our story even though you
do not write them in your book
It is the man who took time to scrape you from the pavement,
stood with you while he picked you up
It is the lady who asked you if you are ok while she gives you a
concerned heartfelt look
The neighbours that grounded you with real talk, while the
world seemed like a place of what the fuck
Your boss who sat with you when your world was crumbling
She listened to your cries through your mumbling
She told you, 'It would take time and it would take all of your
strength.'
It is the stranger who sat quietly with you as you sat there all
alone on a bench
It is the taxi drivers who get you home safely when you are
flooding the seats of their car
With tears of remorse from your drinking, while you do not
even know who you are
It is your friends who still love you when you are not you, but
they know that you are still inside somewhere
It is the teachers who say that you are failing class, and they do
not want you to because they really care
The shopkeeper says 'you do not need this stuff because they
see it is making you ill
They are thinking of your wellbeing, above the thought of
filling their own till
It is your key worker who talks you through your cravings
Because they see a person who they think is worth saving
Strangers at meetings when you are shy and do not know how
to use your voice
The people say there are two paths here, but ultimately, it is
your choice....
It is the people who you forget to mention
They gave you tough love with the right intention
It is the nurses and the doctors that place you on a drip
What say you can come back, and this is just a little slip
The people who you forget to write into your end chapter

They played the biggest big part in your happy ever after

TAXI DRIVER MAN (BOSS)

Hey, taxi driver man
I'm going to cry in your car because I can
I'm going to fall into your taxi out of the bar
And flood the back seats of your car
In fact, I may even tell you my life story
While you're thinking, 'drunken girl, jeez you bore me
I may even lose my phone
Right under the car seat, you know, that forgotten zone
Yaa know what? Forget it, oh jeez
While I'm losing my phone, I may as well lose my keys
'Hey boss, come on, I won't tell. Let me smoke a quick fag'
You might lose your license, but I'm still going to nag
Then I'm going to ask you to go to the shop
Cuz I've ran out of tot
You can wait while I browse and choose
I wouldn't like to be in your shoes
Anyway, taxi driver man, I'm back in
If you are interested, I picked pink gin
So then drop me home, got what I need
I'm paying u the mileage, not your fake made, up greed
Really, he's a Councillor dealing with the tears
Jeeze, he must have seen some sights through his years
Crazy little taxi man, I won't remember your face
I'll crawl out of your taxi, and you'll think what a disgrace
Il pulls out make up covered change
Leave your car with you thinking, wow, that girl was strange

Chapter Twelve

The Hostel System

I lived in a hostel when I was sixteen and then eighteen. I got my first home after that process. The first time I went in, I fell in love with the boy from the hostel down the road. I say, boy, he was twenty-one, I was sixteen.

I think his fake Lacoste tracksuit and the lovely aroma of stale weed pulled me in his direction. This may amaze you now, so hold on to your seats, but that never actually worked out (I know, right), and on the outside, we looked like a scene from Romeo and Juliet. Anyhow, I came back through the Hostel system at eighteen.

I did a few soul-destroying telesales jobs here and there. Still, my main passion was being a support worker and helping others find homes for themself. I got to see both sides of the fence. You are stuck in a catch-22 situation when you live in a hostel. The rent is much higher in hostels because you have a keyworker there, yet you have far less than if you had your own home or tenancy.

You must share facilities with people you may not like, and it feels like being in prison. If you went to work, you couldn't afford the rent, so you are locked in a cycle of signing on and mixing with other dole dossers.

Now the organisation I went through was up to a good standard, but some of the homes/ hostels are not fit for purpose. If you didn't go in with an alcohol or drug addiction, the likely hood is that you would be leaving with one.

St Basils are for sixteen to twenty-five-year-olds, and when I went through the system, it was a different era, there was more funding, and I got to do some wonderful things. I got to perform my poetry at the REP Theatre, The Drum, and Orange Studio's our voices felt heard. It was those experiences that planted the seed for me eventually to set up my own Community interest company. However, I also saw the other side of things as a support worker. I worked for a couple of different agencies, and the difference in the level of service and accommodation is noticeable.

If you think of homelessness as a revolving door, each time someone comes back through the system, they get lowered down the ladder. I have worked in the hostels that everyone has heard of, like the YMCA and Shelter. I've been a floating support worker for an agency where I wouldn't let my dog stay, let alone another human being.

I worked in this one hostel when I was twenty-three. I was pregnant with my daughter then, and it was located in Birmingham a place called Mosely, which I had always thought of as posh. After working there, I soon realised it was not. Where I used to go out on a night out, there was, but just a stone's throw down the road, it was rife with prostitution, heroin, and homelessness. I wrote this poem about one of the girls who lived in one of the hostels.

Black Teeth

Her crooked teeth are black
Can't be scrubbed off, though, they are stained from the crack
She wonders off falling into the night
She might be a crackhead, but she is quite polite
Appears around two or Three
Bloodshot eyes and blood around her knee
A mumbling, slurring young wreck
With love bites covering her bony neck
Wonder which punter did that?
How desperate will she have to be to go back?
Her top is torn must have got ripped
Her second-hand jeans were still unzipped
Her boyfriend, if that is what I must call him, looks glad
Ignoring the experience that his girl just had
Holds his hand out, expecting to see bags
His fingers turned yellow from all the cheap fags
She is unaffected or seems to be unaware
That she abuses her body without a care
In some kind of trap
She has been there too long there no going back
Her eyes are empty; they do not show her soul
She relies on punters, and her Tuesday dole
Scraping through life each day, she must score
Wrecking her body, longing for nothing more
When she sees herself in the mirror
She is turning transparent, getting thinner and thinner
If she listened, I would help
She would rob my purse, I have no doubt
I would not judge her; that is her addiction
She is not in court; that is not her conviction
However, it would hurt; it would doubt my trust
She would look me in the eye though and know I have her
sussed
I know though it is just a means to an end
She sees my purse, not a friend
Anything to catch that high, another tale, another lie
Anything for that end goal

That leaves her empty and takes her soul

When writing this, I did not realise that I had an addiction bubbling under the service that would eventually rip my life into a thousand pieces. I will go into that in a little while, but I want to take you back to that hostel.

I used to have to do the late shift there. Honestly, I had always thought I was streetwise. I used to drink over the park with friends in freezing conditions and get into scraps here and there, but if I am truthful, I was scared working there.

I had to patrol the building every hour to ensure nothing untoward was going on. Walking up and down the landings, there were three floors. Just me against potentially fifty women. These women had done time in prison like it was a walk in the park and were what people may have labelled as the scum of the earth.

They prostituted themselves to get their fix. They begged, borrowed, and stole. I remember getting ready to work once, and my cousin asked me, 'Why do you go and work with those scumbags? Why do you even bother to try to help them?'

I just looked her straight in the eye and said, 'so was I a scumbag then when I lived in them?'

What people do not realise when they see these women prostituting themselves and taking heroin daily is that this lifestyle, they are living came from childhood trauma.

I got to see that, though, as a key worker. One of the ladies I worked with was pregnant, and that child would get taken from her the moment it was born in the hospital.

When she was a young child, her parents sold her into a paedophile ring, and she was given drugs to sedate her and make her comply with the needs of grown men with ill intentions. As a woman now, she is addicted to a substance that eats at her from the inside out.

She prostitutes her body to get a fix. She will be in and out of this hostel system unless she is given a stint in rehab, counselling for her childhood trauma, and a shit ton of money piled into her recovery for the rest of her life.

She is a statistic!

She will never get to love her own children because the people who should have protected and loved her sold her to the vilest people in society. So, while she gets arrested for prostituting HER body to feed the fix imposed upon her uninvited as a child, she gets labelled. She gets arrested while the beasts who pay for her services return to their vanilla marriages at the end of the day. They walk around with no bell around their neck.

Before I worked there, I had a narrow-minded view about the women labelled the dregs of society. When I run workshops in schools, I ask the young people who is worse.

A woman prostituting her body to feed her addiction to a drug that got enforced upon her without consent. Or a young influencer who marries a 70-year-old man who wipes his arse with cash, and she takes selfies on his Yacht?

It gets them thinking, that is for sure.

During my time working at that hostel, THREE women died. I was there for FOUR months.

One died from sniffing lighter fluid. The other was so intoxicated she fell down the stairs and landed funny.

One died of a heroin overdose.

That hostel never made it into the news because it was normal.

I got picked up from there by a taxi driver once, and I was about four months pregnant. I told him I was a worker because the taxi drivers exploited the girls the most.

He took the definition of the word worker wrong and started driving into this dodgy-looking park. I was mortified and petrified at the same time.

Luckily, I showed him my badge, and he realised his mistake, but I thought, imagine what that must feel like. However, I guess by the time you are at the point of doing that to feed your addiction, nothing really feels like anything anymore, just high, chasing high, coming down from high. Repeat.

There may be transactions and interactions exchanged to get you through that cycle. Still, they are just obstacles you must go through to reach the goal of the high of oblivion of numbness. I used to get money from the kitty on Friday nights and do a little spread for the women.

I knew they would not be spending their money on food. We had a couple of karaoke nights, and it was wholesome fun. I saw them as humans with thoughts and feelings. They saw that I did, so their barriers went down.

I left that job, though, because I worried for the safety of my unborn child, not from the women's actions, but I had to get the bus back late at night. I feared the men that patrolled the area looking for desperate women selling their souls.

If I am honest with myself, the likelihood of them recovering is slim. I would imagine many more deaths have happened in that hostel, and I would imagine they were put down as cycle statistics.

I never ever dealt with my childhood trauma. It was nowhere near as horrific as that, but each person's trauma is personal to them. It could be as simple as divorce, bullying, or fighting your identity/sexuality.

Whatever a person's reason for going into addiction, it obviously negatively impacted them enough to try to numb themselves. So, I always try to listen with empathy, whatever a person's back story. It came back to bite me when my daughter was around one years old. I always had drink-related issues, but none to the point where I could not function.

All those hospital ambulance rides, the severity of them just seemed to go over my head. I never drank when I was pregnant, but when my daughter was about one, the addiction started to take hold of me.

I have found out since being in recovery it is standard that it happens after a woman has a baby, which is crazy because you would think it would be the opposite way around.

It is so much more pressure than when it was just you and your feelings. Now you have a tiny little human you must keep alive, hope, and pray you do not mess them up.

I managed to work as a functioning alcoholic till she was eight, and at that time, I worked at a place called SIFA fireside next to the people who worked for Shelter.

I also got my dream job working for St Basils the organisation I went through as a teen. I also got to work in the place I lived, which was rewarding tremendously. SIFA fireside was a drop-in centre for homeless people, they served food, and people could shower, wash their clothes, get spare clothes, speak with a nurse, or get a place to stay for the night.

This place was for entrenched rough homeless sleepers, which I soon discovered. I could not understand why some of these people who attended here actively chose to sleep on the streets instead of in the hostels we could provide them with.

Remember the part, though, when I said each person who goes through the revolving door, the places get worse each time. Well, some of these people had burnt bridges in some of the hostels, so the ones they got offered were more like squats.

Unregulated providers started setting up and charging a lot in housing benefits because they would say there were housing support key workers that were unregulated and non-existent. This would mean that for a box room, they were sometimes charging housing benefits of £300 in rent a week.

These kinds of homes would be filled with drug users, immigrants, and the people that walked through the door at half four on a Friday saying they were homeless. The feedback we would get from these street sleeper homeless people, was that it was surprisingly safer on the streets than in those places and that there was a sense of community there.

I got a bit annoyed once. I was doing a risk and needs assessment with one rough sleeper, and every ten minutes, he would stop the meeting so he could go outside and drink his cider. This was because it was not allowed on the premises.

(I thought to my self-priorities, right) It was not until I was at my first keyworker meeting to go into rehab when I had to keep breaking it up to swig cheap glens vodka, that I realised why he did that. He wouldn't have gotten to the place if he hadn't, let alone sat down for ten minutes each time.

I loved working there; many people didn't, but this was real front-line stuff. I was so appalled once, we got a call from Birmingham Mental Hospital, they were discharging a woman, and she had no place to live, so they released her to us.

They discharged her in her dressing gown! To sit in a male-dominated place where people had addictions, including sex addictions. She may as well have been a steak on a BBQ for some hungry bears. I know this writing makes me sound anti-male, but I am not. I have lots of positive male role models I look up to. I just wanted to put that here because This is a piece of writing about the system, not against the male population. Where was the compassion?

151

We would get women fleeing DV relationships who repeatedly went around in a circle like the homeless cycle. I would think, just leave him. He doesn't love you. The answer is simple: just take your kids and start a new life.

Until I ended up in a domestic violence relationship and became just a shell of who I was. Going back and forth, a relationship with a narcissist is like repeatedly being in a train crash. Somehow, they convince you it was your fault they drove the train into you, and you end up apologising for making them steam.

People do not seem to realise that all these things go in hand. Unresolved childhood trauma. Addiction, domestic violence, and mental health, equal homelessness. I am missing crime on there, but I cannot relate to that. I did some shoplifting here and there as a youth, but nothing I could write home about enough to connect to that system.

My point is that there is no point in just solving homelessness, because if there is an addiction, the likelihood is that the tenancy will not be sustainable. If there is co-dependency and addiction that ends up with DV, you will end up at the drawing board again.

To be able to write down these words from this perspective, I am one of the lucky ones, one of the ones in the tiny percentage that overcome such hurdles. I so easily could not have been. At one point, I was not going to make it; it was touch and go, and that's what makes me so passionate about wanting to help people still in pain.

I went through years of pain in addiction and put people through years of pain watching me destroy myself. I fled Birmingham eventually, and I was given a place with Bromford.

The fresh start changed my world, the world for my daughter, and my recovery flourished. I was in so much unbearable pain I was at a crossroads, live or die, I wanted to die, but I couldn't do that to my daughter, and I am so lucky that I pushed through and broke the cycle. How many people will not, though?

How many people will go through this revolving door of homelessness? While we only deal with homelessness, we are setting the people up to fail.

Ask ourselves why they are homeless?

If it's domestic abuse, do they need counselling?

Shall we refer to other organisations?

Would self-esteem-boosting workshops help?

Was it sexual abuse?

Is it an addiction?

Do they know of the recovering community?

I've heard of the offender-to-rehab program whereby proleptic re-offenders addicted to heroin are sent to rehab, not prison. Some of those people that went through that system are thriving.

I didn't know there was a community on my doorstep of recovering addicts. Mental health, where can you refer on?

People are too busy to see people and not statistics. Still, by looking deeper into the core of the problem, you stop the revolving door from endlessly turning. Sometimes all it takes is one good key worker, one social worker with a heart. Not just a textbook, one person to say 'I SEE YOU' How crazy, though, that's like Russian roulette on a person's life.

My company is called Been There Done That cic. There are so many other communities interest companies out there. These companies usually are set up by people with lived experience. They know how it feels on the inside and are passionate in a way that people who do not know how it feels just can't be.

Check out your local Community interest companies. You will be surprised how many there are, or think, is there a need for one? Could you, do it? Could someone you know do it? Work together as teams, not against each other, fighting over pots of money. If your end goal is to help people, stop seeing pound signs and lose the moral inventory you set yourself in the first place.

I think it would be great if we did like a celebrity jungle-style hostel experiment called I am a politician, get me out of here, whereby we put the people who set the budgets into some shared houses and some YMCA hostels for thirty days and gave them only universal credit to live on and see how they got on. They get to keep their seat if they don't emerge completely broken.

Pretty fair, I'd say, they get to go in without that weight around their ankle of childhood trauma, labels, stereotypes, and lack of hope, so they are already leaping ahead. That wouldn't work though, because they would know at the end of the 30 days, they would be going back to a life of luxury, claiming sixty thousand pounds back in expenses for eyebrows and doing backhand deals with companies they have a silent investment in.

It has been this way forever the rich get richer while the poor get poorer and are told they are the problem.

Divide and conquer create fear and keep the people humble and held. If you don't jump through the hoops we put in place, we will take away your fundamental human rights. However, we will put through expenses that we could have easily paid ourselves because we quite simply can.

Polish my shoes while you are picking up our leftovers, will you?

If you strip it right down to the education system. Where are the life skills, lessons on credit scores, healthy relationships, and addiction? There may be odd little workshops here and there, but it is outside the curriculum.

I would have received help from learning them, far more than algebra. I can honestly say as a thirty-five-year-old dyslexic adult, I have never used algebra in my life. What about helping young pupils get through their theory tests because their chances of employment open tenfold if they can drive, just a thought?

Some fantastic organisations are out there, though, and that should be acknowledged.

They do help people, look at them like humans, not just statistics, and they shouldn't be tarnished with that brush of hostels are awful, etc.

I have a beautiful home now in a beautiful part of the world provided by Bromford.

This is my little part of heaven, some may think it is just a council house, but to me, it is a world away from where I was, where I was heading to, and how my life would have been if I hadn't of broke the cycle.

This is not bricks and mortar. These walls are for making beautiful sober, happy memories. When the government set universal credit to pay people's rent, it set people up to fail.

If you have an addiction, your rent is not going on rent now, is it? Yet there is a duty of care to house the homeless. So how is that beneficial? because they will just come back through the system, but the government will pay out more money in hostel charges makes zero sense.

If you have mental health issues Bi-Polar, for instance, you cannot control spending on a high, why is this not looked into more?

In domestic violence relationships, are they financially abusive toward them? Give them your rent, or they will break your ribs again, and you can only just cough again without curling up in pain? There should not be a blanket approach because it ends up the same way.

It is like it is designed to keep the lower-class lower class so that they cannot thrive above their station. The cost of living, heating, eating, or rent?

I have been on both sides of the fence, and for things to move forward, there must be change. If you are reading this, though, and you are in a cycle and cannot see a way out, you can, I did, and all the odds were stacked against me.

Use that to fuel your fire instead of letting the ashes crush your spirit. I am going to work hard, and I am going to buy this home one day.

This home will be my daughter's legacy. When people who think, it was just handed to me on a plate read my story, they will realise I survived things they never could get to this point. If it wasn't for housing providers who are there at the end of this cycle, for the people who survive the homeless hunger games, then there wouldn't be hope.

People are quick to judge. Live a day in someone else's shoes before you stamp over their dreams with yours. Eat dried milk noodles and bread from your silver spoons and see how those taste. If you cannot find compassion for the man who sleeps in doorways or the woman who sells her soul, then at least just say nothing. These people are not social projects for you to throw a pound to, so you can upload your bio on social media to say you do charity work. They could have been so many other things and may someday be Free.

Until that day, though, I want them to know, I SEE YOU.

I Know

I know what it's like to stay in random places
Trying to avoid the heartache and the same old faces
I know what it's like to take drugs to numb the pain
To look in the mirror and always feel plain
Being homeless made me feel like I couldn't respect myself
Depression and clouded judgment made me neglect myself
Feeling dirty and when you wash, you still feel unclean
Crying and hurting but no shoulder for you to lean
When I was younger, I wanted to be a midnight raver
On most typical days, though, I couldn't even afford a day
saver
Worrying about gas and electric
My life turned out that way. I didn't expect it
I vowed to move away from my 16th birthday
I heard that hostels were bad from experience and hearsay
I didn't want to live on the streets. I couldn't possibly stay at
home
When I left home, I had no material possessions to take with me
like a tv, DVD bedsheets or a phone
So, I'm going to tell you about the dangers and the
consequences
How vital them 20ps become and those 50 pence's
Each letter you get sent is a bill
Making you ill
But sometimes you have to hit rock bottom so you can turn
your life back around
Let out those tears out but try to not make a sound
Be brave, be strong don't be afraid to ask for help
Only you can change your life; no one else
Homelessness is painful homelessness is true
It can be a really lonely place and could happen to you.
So never judge the cover of an unread book
You can turn your life around. I did take a look

Chapter Thirteen

There is something I have got to tell you.

I have got to tell you something, and it feels really awkward now because we have got so far down into the book.

I just did not want to put it in here, and I have put it off and put it off. But, to understand addiction, you have to understand the behaviours. Well, before I ever had a substance addiction, I had an eating disorder that the doctors call bulimia nervosa.

Honestly, I am more ashamed of that than I am of the drinking.

Although it has not caused as much havoc as alcohol, it's messed my body up.

People do not understand it because they think you would be stick thin to have bulimia and that I am not.

I was, though, when I first got it at the age of fourteen, twenty years ago (wow, that's a long time to have a binge and purge for)

Our bodies are clever little things, or big things (whatever smart arse).

That's just me talking to the voice that cracked that joke in my head.

Ha-ha, a hilarious fat joke while we are talking about bulimia to lighten the mood. That would be great. Then people may remember the joke and forget all about that magnitude of a secret I've had forever, because it is starting to feel a bit tense now.

I can understand why I got the eating disorder in the first place; my parents had split custody when I was a child.

My Mom is thin and healthy and loves hiking and carrots, looking after herself, and has been known to rock up at mine with a potato in her bag, I kid you not, for me to cook so she can have a baked potato. I am not saying this in a derogatory way. I wish at times I had that level of discipline. (Or a vegetable I could use at any time, should I need to defend myself against sheep or aggressive pigeons or something, have a potato you baaing bastards, and shut the fuck up, will ya,'

My dad likes food. My Nanny Win was on my dad's side of the family. She would do big portions of food, puddings, buttery toast, sugary tea, and a biscuit tin that sang my name whenever I went around.

Food was celebrated with junk and yummy stuff, while at my mom's, it was healthy.

Two different extremes.

My Mom is also a vegetarian, I was when I was a child, but it was more, so I could impress her than understand it all.

The first time I ate meat again was a McDonald's burger, just before we were about to go to a party, where the rule was, if you're not taking pills, you are not coming in.

I took the pills, obvs, but oh my god the burger played havoc with my stomach. It was too rich after not eating meat for so many years.

That was a super embarrassing scenario while everyone else was having fantastic trips, (I remember one of the lads seeing the laughing cow from the cheese adverts floating out the window)

I was shitting my bloody kegs.

Everyone was in too much of a world of their own to notice, but for me, it wasn't the best experience of taking ecstasy, it definitely didn't stop me taking more though.

I actually got the nickname FBT for a while. It stands for Fat Bastard Turkey. My Friends weren't calling me a fat bastard, but my dad is a ginger, and the Austin powers movie was just out, so my mates would do the impressions of the ginger man, saying it was my dad. (Sorry, dad)

Me and my mate Boggy he got that nickname because when he was little, his hair used to spike out like a bog brush aha. (he'll kill me if he reads this)

He is 35 now, and people still call it him. It just kind of stuck.

Anyhow, we decided it was time to do a run-out for some booze from our local Michaels. We were already pissed at this point and probably about 14/15.

Well, I had fallen out with my mom then. I was still rebelling after trying the burger the week before, against vegetarianism.

Well, in my drunken stupor, I tried to rob some alcohol but got an overwhelming urge to nick some of that turkey ham shite.

Safe to say, we got caught and surrounded by those who owned the shop.

They said, 'give it back to us, and we won't call the police,' so boggy is handing over what he had, and then there's me handing back a pack of turkey ham.

Boggy just looks at me and laughs like, 'what the fuck, why did you rob the turkey ham for?'.

Anyway, the name stuck Fat Bastard Turkey. No one calls it me anymore thank God, because, how do you explain that nickname?

Without looking like crazed turkey ham eating hulk.

They still call bog boggy, though, so aha.

Ok, so I side-tracked again.

That led to the feeling of guilt and shame and hating the way I looked. The whole healthy, if you're hungry, eat a grape vibe to fancy some lard confusion. (Just to clarify, I never ate grapes dipped in lard) I'm not painting that much of a good picture here, am I?

Most fourteen-year-old girls hate the way that they look, but I was chubby when I was in year six.

I got bullied. I don't think the weight helped.

Then I went to this senior school where you could not afford to get bullied, so I reinvented myself. It was the era of tracksuits, Rockport, and those gold chains with the rag dolls on end. We would glue our hair down with that cheap blue gel and a nit comb to create the slap, as we called it. Basically, your hair stuck to your forehead with gel.

There were many playground school gate fights, and I was in lots of them. I didn't want to be labelled the tubby one, so it took hold of me, the bulimia.

Most teenagers have a lack of self-esteem. Your hormones fluctuate like a tornado from one week to the next.

I had moved in full-time with my dad by that point, lots of families have complex dynamics and situations, but this book isn't intended to slag off my upbringing or place blame anywhere else, so it wouldn't be suitable. All is well now, so to dive into the past and trudge everything up. Just isn't worth it, I was no angel that's for sure.

(I have a good relationship with most of my immediate family now, and that is how I would like it to stay.)

I have done that, obviously, via my therapy, rehab, etc. But it doesn't need to be in the public domain. This is merely trying to help others with bulimia, any kind of eating disorder, or self-harm, understand that they are not alone.

A lot of addicts start with this, not all, but it is known within the rooms. When I say rooms, I mean AA or NA meetings.

I let boys treat me like utter garbage because I felt so low about myself. I allowed people to take advantage of me, in the hope one day I'd get a boyfriend, they would love me, and all my problems would be solved. News flash, most teenage boys are just horny little shits, and a tubby girl with low self-esteem is bloody gold dust to up those tallies on the board.

Then I got thin, not super night, about a size eight, which is super thin for my build. I am fourteen now. In an ideal world, I'd like to be a small-toned size twelve, but that's a book for another day aha. Body blitz with Beth or something cheesy like that.

Bulimia is something I battled with for years and went to the doctors about for years. Before I got pregnant with my Belle, I was on Prozac, which was absolutely vile.

Apparently, large doses of it are supposed to blast the bulimia out of you. They kept me on it because it was safe to take while pregnant.

If you are on Prozac and reading this book, I just want to say if it is working for you, fantastic, I am glad it is helping, but it never agreed with me, not one bit.

I strongly believe now, looking back, I had antenatal depression on top of my other depression. I think those tablets messed up my feelings and made me numb. They would give me blackouts. Those tablets were the devil. When mixed with alcohol, they make you vile.

I have not physically put my fingers down my throat for a long time (oh, that just feels so horrible to even type).

I will be honest, though; it has never entirely gone away. If I overeat or binge my head absolutely hammers me.

Sometimes I am just sick because my body has purged over two decades. I didn't keep a Christmas dinner down for over fifteen years. I have thrown up in endless public toilets and wretched so bad I have pissed myself.

I get frustrated and anxious if I've binged and cannot get rid of it with a purge, snappy and short-tempered because the shame is starting to engulf me. (Well, what does that remind you of ay)

It is all pointless because your body just stores the calories when they enter your mouth. It gets clever and learns to cling to them before they go out. That's why you end up over weight not underweight in the end.

You strip yourself of vitamins, dehydrate yourself, and open yourself up to missed periods, infertility, and much more, so why do we do it.

CONTROL.

I was delivering a class the other day on fears. People said heights, the depth of the ocean, a roller coaster, a very fast spider, Prison, ending back in addiction, or a loved one dying.

What do all these things have in common?

On the top of a ladder, you are not in CONTROL of if it falls.

In the ocean's depths, you are not in CONTROL of the current, what is beneath you, or where you may end up.

A roller coaster, you are not in CONTROL of its speed, if it breaks down, or if you piss yourself in fear.

A spider dashes, we are not in CONTROL of our surroundings because it can run and hide, and we won't know where it will be. We might swallow it in our sleep, or it may have a million babies.

Prison, not in CONTROL, which is an obvious one.

Addiction, we were not in CONTROL of our own bloody minds. It got hijacked by an asshole.

A loved one dying, we are not in CONTROL of fate, Mother nature, another person's thoughts or feelings, suicide, cancer, the clock ticking, the list is endless.

So, what is binging and purging?

It is losing control, a frenzy, a mania, an overwhelming urge to eat all the fridge, all that you know is bad for you.

Feeling amazing as you eat, the euphoria of the sugar rushes the taste, the naughtiness.

When you are full of food and shame, you purge. What are you trying to do? Gain back control.

161

So even though, scientifically, you know this method doesn't work, it's another form of self-harm, self-loathing, having your cake and eating it... (Then throwing it back up)

Then thinking, 'oh shit, I shouldn't have done that.'

This can affect our mood considerably.

Hangry, that's a different kind of vile.

Getting food, buzzing can't wait yum yum

Eating all the food (oh fuck well-done tubby)

Everyone does this to themself in one form or another, not just with food but exercise, gaming, binge-watching tv, etc. If we don't exercise enough, we feel shit, but we get locked into a series on Netflix we binge it for two days straight.

We feel shit, we train harder than usual to push through the guilt etc. then we tire ourselves out to the point of loathing the exercise.

I do not want to talk about all this too much, because this has been an exceedingly difficult chapter for me to write. But I want to be truthful, and writing a book without one of my biggest skeletons in the closet is not truthful, its sugar coating the truth.

But what if they all think I am a nut job?

The addictions are one thing, the depression another. Throw an eating disorder into the mix, they are going to think I am tornado, bat shit, bullshit crazy.

Do you want to know the truth, though?

Most things go hand in hand.

For example, when I was a homeless support worker, we would do a risk and needs assessment.

You would find they didn't just wake up homeless. It was either hand in hand with mental health/addiction/domestic abuse etc. You know all this, though from the last chapter.

Have you ever stopped and chatted with a homeless person just five minutes of your time?

They are just hurt humans who have most likely been chewed up and spat out of the system so many times that they are a number, a statistic, not a person.

Some people are so stuck in their ways you may not be able to help them now. There is nothing wrong with planting seeds of hope, though. If you know places that can help them, write it down and hand it to them on a piece of paper.

That's far more valuable than money. That is why I created the anthology I did previously, Our Little Book of Hope, to give to homeless people.

Could I tackle all my problems at once though, no. when I first went into rehab, I came off everything, said I didn't need my antidepressants anymore, I didn't even take my vitamin B and Thiamine. After two weeks I was like I'm cured I don't need rehab any more or anti-depressants I'm fine.

I was not fine.

I relapsed after 6 weeks and during that relapse I did worse things than I had in all the previous years of drinking to myself because the shame hit me so much harder, I thought I had it sussed, that I was fixed, that I was free, that it was over, and I could just go back to drinking like a normal human again.

In 2 weeks, my world spiralled apart to the depths of despair.

So, when I actually went back into rehab and listened more and was open to more. I realised I would have to fix one thing at a time. Starting with the one that was doing the most damage.

That was the alcohol, the alcohol was going to kill me I have no doubt about that, whether it be a drunken accident, suicide or the long haul liver failure it was going to kill me.

So, I've started with that, then the mental health, then the negative relationship I had with my self-worth, then the bad relationships, now the bulimia. If I tried to do it all at once it would have been too much. I had to dissect it all piece by piece, pull myself apart like a smashed-up jigsaw, then bit by bit find new pieces that fitted much better.

It was funny, once, I was working in a rehab centre, and saw my book on the side, and noticed a bit of the bottom had been ripped off. Someone had used my bloody Book of Hope for spliff roach; its irony just ticked me.

I did not want to be a statistic. I certainly did not want Belle to be an addict's daughter statistic.

Here are a couple of poems that will help you understand the places my mind has been at times, not anymore, but when I was locked in a cycle.

Also, I wrote a poem about statistics which seems quite fitting.

Bulimia

I sit there stuffing my face
It always ends up in the same place
Eat, purge, then eat, then purge
Not even hungry, but still got the urge
At least I'm not drinking though
Like whiplash, I dash, eat, purge, and throw
Up
I'm on a binging spree, so don't interrupt
It's like a mania
They gave it a name, bulimia...
Then added nervosa
I just know it makes me feel in control when I release it back
out
Even if I wanted to keep it in the voices well, urges would
shout
Get it out, get it out
Cuz after the binging comes the shame and that uneasy feeling
Tubs of ice cream, packs of chocolate bars, sugar rush to reach
the ceiling
Lactose intolerant but had cream
Like I can find any way I can to be mean
To myself I'm eating purging eating purging
Tired from the lack of vitamins
It all started out to feel in control, but like most addictions, it
now controls me.
Like the drink used to, so I guess I'm not actually free
The eating purging cycle is like drinking being hungover one
You need to eat to survive, though not like a drink, u don't get a
buzz from a chocolate bar Hun
You do release endorphins from purging, though, and it's that
high for a second u are chasing
I've tried replacing
These obsessions with the gym and then a swim
But then I come out from the swimming baths starving
With new justifications for the junk that I know I'll eat and then
purge and then eat and then purge
Even when I try to resist that urge

To eat those mars, all the chocolate bars, the caramel Twix
At least I'm not drinking, though, but I'm far from fixed

Depression

How do I change the pattern of a lifetime and change my
mind's dimensions?
How do I flip around my thoughts and send them in different
directions?
Break the cycle yea that's obvious but how?
I thought it was working out alright; I've realised just now

So, shall I give up everything I've been doing for so long?
I guess I'm going to have to. I'll be fine; I am strong
So today is the first day I have realised
It's got to be done no time for compromise

Yea, but it's gone on for so many years it's the only way I know
Well, it has not worked out so far; the evidence is on show
Alright, then, but where can I go for help?
Well, you should look in the mirror and start with yourself

Good point, but the mirror is exactly what I've been avoiding
The pictures though they, can be, so soul destroying
But if you sort it out, then you won't have to think like this
What if I fail? With you, it's always I can't, I can't what if!

You read about the side effects, didn't you? Just look at what
you're doing to yourself?
You can get really ill one day; it's the fault of no one else
I've tried to fight it before, well clearly not hard enough
Well, you try and be inside my mind, and then you'll see that
this is tough

What are you on about? I deal with this every single day
Trying to keep those urges at bay
You just don't listen; you block out me
But what would I know? I'm just your BODY

One Day

One day I'll make you proud you will be glad I'm your
daughter
And the tears that we have cried will just be wasted water
The puffy eyes will be replaced with laughter
The bad times the before that led to the afters

I will show that my brain has been bulging
With fresh money, we will be indulging
Bad girl has gone good with all of these ideas
I will ignore the put-downs and spiteful sneers

Although I'm not in it for the money
Floating above water will seem kind of funny
For years my life has been sinking
Now I'm floating cause I'm finally thinking

I want to change my life and the life of others
Naughty daughters and angry mothers
Fuming fathers and miss lead sons
You're not alone or the only ones

Making a positive out of a negative is not easy
Turning your life around is hard; please believe me
You feel like you are chasing butterflies that are impossible to
catch
But anything is possible; just look at the way they hatch

You can read books to fuel your brain
Or just muddle along, leaving your mind plain
Look, I'll admit I didn't stick it in college
I just survive on my instinct and general knowledge

Everyone has a talent depends on whether you put it to use
You can dwell on the past or give your life a boost
I used to be quite happy just chilling in the pub
But now I'm determined to make my life good

Shallow

I am not shallow like this world we live in
The one I long to succeed in
Like the ocean, my pain runs deep
Your face always corrupts the way that I sleep
When did this world become a fight?
It's no longer plain like black and white
Soon the day fades, releasing the night
Your voice overrides my fading eyesight
For you, I am grieving
For you, my heart is continuously bleeding
Under my eyes, a pale green bruise?
The skin under them, tired because of the salt tears I have used
The heat dries my skin; it's so dry, almost crisp
And the scars only deepen, almost reaching my wrist
When you told me you loved me, I'm sure you were pissed
I saw your face through the purple mist
You called me treacle and said 'it was because I was sweet'
You adored my body, my hair, the soles of my feet
A dark cloud covers you. Am I the silver lining?
A dark cloud circles me, only increasing my pining
My fingertips shake, and my senses wake.
I'm crippled by the thoughts my mind likes to make
I wander alone, searching for your face
I wonder alone at a snail-like pace
I am burning, sun scorching, fresh freckles appearing
My hearts beating faster to you. Am I nearing?
I am dreaming, reaching out my hand
I am melting into grains turning into sand
I'm still holding onto this pain
I will wait until I'm one single grain
I cannot see through the sandstorm
Your face appears I am reborn
Your face fades sun darkening my skin shades
I am yearning time ticking clock turning
You are the one that I love the most
So, appear from the storm and reveal your ghost

Depression

I locked up the thoughts in a music box
But one of the demons picked the lock
All of the shadows and black clouds are chilling on my bed
All of the demons and bad memories have camped out in my head
My fingertips are frozen, black clouds blocking the sun so they will not warm up
I see their reflections through my eyes, and I can tell that they are stuck
They scream lullabies; they appear in my nightmares; they darken my childhood
They play mind games with me and spike my happy thoughts when I'm good
All of these tarnished thoughts were locked in the box and put far away
Have found a way out and came out to play
They confuse me and turn on my water taps
Playing with the strings in my mind refusing to relax
They cover my eyes with snakeskin and make my stomach churn like gone off cheese
They fall out of my mind with my tears and fly out of my mind when I sneeze
Singing and dancing and having an uninvited party in my mind
And when the demons are hung over, that's when they are unkind
I keep on searching for the key. I have no hope
And they climb into my mind on ladders swinging through my mind on a rope
I can't put faces to them
It's like someone has glued them
Sitting on black clouds glued to the cells in my brain
The demons, the black clouds, the dreams sending me insane
Please let me lock them back up, as I'm all on edge
Contemplating jumping off the window ledge
I'm all jittery, confused, and fidgety
Please lock them back up so I can claim back my sanity

Where are you now?

They say "out of sight, out of mind"
There are just the words of someone being kind
Implanted until your face, I find
I will never walk away and leave your memory behind

Out of sight, the pain only deepens until I am way too deep
Your face and your voice then appear in my sleep
Tears trickle like raindrops until I finally weep
Then its Monday again, time to face a fresh week
Where are you now?

I will spend my empty days searching
A glimmer of hope, then it's back to just hurting
Days pass while the healer is turning
I fall to pieces, trying to deal with this yearning

Angels appear with your face in my dreams
Is that a sign? I don't know what it means
I try to sew myself up as I rip at the seams
I search for a shoulder as my heavy head leans

Where are you now?

Silence swirls around with the crystal-like air
I imagine you here smelling my hair
I look through the mirrors and try to see if you're there
But my reflection stares blankly without a care

A sound like your voice makes my fingertips shake
The thought of your eyes, the feel of your face
The smell of your skin, my senses wake
The loss that I feel I don't think I can take
Where are you now?

Chapter Fourteen

(I think, fuck knows, I'm losing count)

Nothing ever starts out bad, like a domestic violence relationship. If they greeted you with a punch in the face, then you are not likely to continue that relationship, are you?

There is a grooming process. During that time, everything is glorious, like you're walking on air.

You get loved bombed, well, in my case, booze bombed.

Well, it's a bit like addiction before it was ever bad. It wasn't just good. It was a level of euphoria of escapism of freedom you could never explain.

That first sip of alcohol that gave you an alter ego will be what you forever chase for the rest of your time in active addiction.

Remember what I said? when I went into rehab

I felt like I was a fifteen-year-old in a thirty-something's body.

I thought it would be fitting to start this chapter back there.

So, let's do that thing real authors do when they set the scene.

(Was that a little bit of self-doubt there, Beth hmm caught you)

It is a Friday night at the park. We used to congress over a park called Oaklands (now half of it has been turned into a shopping centre)

Anyhow, we had stood outside the shop for ages and managed to get some poor passers-by to go into the shop. To get us 10 sovereigns a bottle of vodka and half a basket full of that cheap booze they used to sell in the bargain basket, that was out of date and had all bits floating around in it, but for 29p, we ignored that factor. Honestly, back then, I would have drunk petrol if it got us pissed. We used to drink this cider called 3 hammers, brutal shite it was.

I never wagged that day in school because Friday was the day, I wanted to get my booze money, so I would clean the house and be a model teenage daughter.

When I think of Joe, I think so fondly back to those days. He always used to sing, 'thirteen is an unlucky number.'

We would hover around the swan centre because his brother Billy had a job in the butchers there, he had a friend called Moo Head, and we would just sit there stoned, making Mooing noises.

He had an infectious laugh. Joe was beautiful not just on the outside but inside too. I think Joe was a bit misunderstood. He was like me in some ways. He would drink for confidence because he was shy.

He was kind though, in nature and had a good heart.

I think of Joe so often, that I wouldn't have my Belle if it wasn't for bumping into them years later, but we will go on that later.

It was hard that day to pick what tracksuit to wear. All I ever wanted was a Lacoste tracksuit. You were part of the elite if you had the Lacoste tracksuit to go with the Rockport's.

I never had Rockport's. I had Lacoste shoes. Looking back, they were so bloody ugly, but on the rare occasions I went to school, you had to own either Rockport or Lactose, or you may as well of just lived in a bin.

The likely hood is I would have slapped my hair down to my head with blue 69p gel. I had a perm as a teenager. Another nickname (big worm with the big perm) from the film Friday.

I have always loved curly hair.

I would use so much hair moose it would crunch and so much hair spray even a blizzard wouldn't have moved it.

Talking of moose, makeup was about an inch thick, and the dream matt moose was like cement. For a while, blue mascara was in fashion, none of this contour and stick your eyebrows to your face.

For some reason, it was also fashionable to pluck your eyebrows to within an inch of their life. I shaved mine off and used to draw little thin things on. (You were straight out of luck if it rained.)

Sometimes, on a Friday night, no exaggeration, there could be up to about seventy of us setting fires to keep warm.

You just do not see that anymore. We live in quite a different world now. Everyone gets offended. We wouldn't have lasted five minutes now. We were ruthless little shits. (Not nasty to people, just causing teenage havoc, really)

This millennial world has its pros and cons.

It was in fashion to be a bit of a geezer bird, and after getting bullied for that year 6 puppy fat, I would just fight anyone by this point. Which is not always a great idea after a bottle of vodka.

Joe and I got arrested once, because some guy was being seedy at the bar, so I chucked my drink over him, and he hit me, and Joe saw, so a big fight happened in the pub. I had a zebra coat on.

The police came, and we all got nicked. I couldn't really hide in the zebra coat, and Joe was just sticking up for me. But that's what he was like. He would always stick up for his friends.

We had some of the best times of our lives over that park, and I still speak to my main group of girls now, and I will love them forever.

We have had many ups and downs over the years, but that group of friends are the only people on this earth who can really understand what our youth was like.

We all had stuff going on at home, which made us like magnets to each other, and we all became our own version of a family.

At the time, we had a group of lads we hung around with that we just loved so much. We bumped into some of them years later, a night out up Solihull (that's what I was talking about earlier). Belle's father chilled with them, and that's how I met him. On a night out, he was there.

Joe was my friend, and unfortunately, he passed away due to committing suicide a couple of years ago, and it really knocked me for six., I dreamt about him the night it happened, and it blew my mind because I had not seen him for years.

To me, he was such a massive part of my childhood. He went to my infant and junior school.

We had so many memories, and I will always cherish them.

My message to him and my other friend who passed this year and anyone who feels that way is. You are loved. This world will not be a better place without you in it. There is nothing that cannot be fixed. I am sorry. I never knew. You are missed, and you will be missed more than you will ever know. I love you.

I wish there was more support for male suicide, or any form of suicide, as I know what it feels like to be in so much pain you do not want to live. You convince yourself that the world will be a better place without you.

I wanted to mention them in this book to acknowledge them and what a big part of my childhood they both were.

I hope this may help someone and that it may bring some comfort to their families.

After we were all pissed on a Friday night, we would chant this song we made up.

I get drunk every Friday night
If my dad knew, give him a fright
Sometimes we end up in a fight.
If you want to go, then that's all right
I'm getting sick of all of this.
Every weekend I get pissed.
Why do that when we can just smoke a spliff?
It's all right...

Talking of weed, that's in that song. We got stoned literally every single day. We would sub weed or put our school dinner money together.

I do not know how on earth I that did, because if I even smell weed now, it makes me feel dizzy.

We would just literally always be high, lessons in school were always so much more fun, I remember once we nicked this teachers chocolate bar when we had the munchies. Tasted so much better because it was hers.

In P.E I would get barred from going for playing up and my punishment was to have to go with the lads. I was buzzing I got to perve on all the fit lads playing football stoned out my head.

I like CBD, but obviously, you do not get a buzz from that.

We also used to hang around a place called the swan market. They had a car park and an old loading bay that was great for sheltering from the British elements. It was also good fun getting chased by the security guard if we wanted to cause some Havok.

Here is my poem if you want to get a feel of the place.

Our Little Shit Hole, the Swan

When we were younger used to climb up the long rusty steps of
the swan
To the top floor of the car park with rizla to get one on
We would spend hours drinking in the loading bay
Cold nights that surfaced after spending time in the cafe all-day
We would terrorise the security guard, rob some cheese to get
chase
He couldn't keep up with our teenage pace
Me n Kezza B once hid in the toilets n got locked in there after
closing
We got caught, though, so we fly-kicked the door off and were
hot foot toeing
We loved the shitty shops that felt like home
Like a time, warp, entering that IN MARKET shop zone
That old horse by the toilets that had been there about twenty
years
The tot shops outside would sell gone-off beers
The little chemists that id run to after a hair dye disaster
Usually getting toner, wasn't quite yet a bleaching master
The old block buster's right by the island opposite the shape S
Those days in that rusty shit hole were simply the best
Remember sitting on the benches planning our trip to
Earlswood woods
Deciding who we could get to go in the shop and load up on all
the goods
That lurky tot shop used to sell vodka with weed seeds in
Pink was normally the colour you would see me in
On hot days over Oaklands, there was a little shop opposite that
sold weed
We would stock up on the space raiders tip tops and roisters for
our feed
We were little shits that hung round causing mayhem, lurking
around in pizza pan
Now kids just piss about doing ticktock while we were on our
toes from the police. We ran
I think it was maybe the era we grew up in tracksuits, zog, and
drum n base

The girls these days get to chill and look pretty, while u
couldn't see the eyebrows on my face
We were young, we were foolish, we were carefree, and the
place where it all begun
Was a place that is only there in memory, a rusty little shithole
called the SWAN

I went to a school called Cockshut hill, but I got kicked out just before my exams. I was in all the top sets in year seven, but as my behaviour deteriorated, so did my grades, and I would get moved down to the lower classes each year due to my behaviour disrupting the class.

Home life was rocky, but as I said before, this book is not about that. Due to some of those circumstances, I moved into a hostel at 16 and eventually had my own flat as a teenager in a place called Chelmsley Wood. I loved that flat. It was in a high rise, but it was massive. I was one of the only people in my friendship circle to have my own place, so therefore that home became party central.

When I first moved in there, I didn't have a clue, my friend Jenna and I painted the whole entire kitchen in gloss paint. I didn't know you could get different types of paint.

Jenna's Dad, Steve, was an absolute legend. Sadly, he's passed away, so I want to acknowledge him and say how incredibly proud he would be of you, Jenna. Steve decided to nickname me Blue Waffle, a glorious nickname to have, and just to clarify, I've never had it. Nonetheless, it was amusing, I actually wrote in his memorial book love from blue waffle, which may not be appropriate, but I am sure he would have found the funny side. I also know it will tickle Jenna when she reads this part because she used to find it hilarious. She most likely made the rumour up aha.

One time I came home pissed from a night out, put my hand in pink paint and did all pink hand prints up the wall. I woke up like, what the fuck.

I seemed to have a running theme with paint over the years, I used to take it out on my bathroom in my old house, the one that it all got really bad in. I nicknamed it my bipolar bathroom. When I was happy, I painted it all in silver glitter paint, but then during one of my depression moments, I painted it all in black.

Anyway, back to the good times.

We had moved on from just drinking over the park, and it was more of the era of ecstasy and cocaine and our very favourite MDMA.

One night in the Highrise, we continued the verse to our song.

Now we are older, things have changed.
We take drugs, but they are not the same.
Ecstasy and the cocaine
So many drugs messing with my brain

We had stopped hanging around with the lads over the park and met a new group of lads we called the Dudes. We called them the dudes because they were indie and quirky and liked Kings of Leon, oasis, and guitars, not so much tracksuits and drum and base.

Those days were some of the best days of my life. Some of the lads from the group and I went over to Ibiza to try and do a season. We were there for about six weeks. It was the start of the recession. We went out there prob a month too early and ran out of money.

I also came back for a guy (stupid, I know)

Prob one of the worst decisions I have ever made, we went around in circles for ten years, and it was like he would be with the whole entire world but me.

It made me feel really worthless, we were friends, but it was very evident that I had feelings for him, that he just did not have for me.

We were friends right up until I went to rehab, but it all went very tits up in a bit of an explosion. In fairness to him, I used to get very drunk because I could not handle my emotions, and then when I was drunk, it would all come out in a barrel of abuse.

Pride, ego, and fear of rejection arc what fed into that cycle.

I would act like I wasn't bothered when he was with other people, even though it used to hurt like hell.

I should have been more honest with myself. I should have protected myself, but there's a whole lot of should of, would of, could of.

I think he did care for me as a friend, but I think rejection is one of the hardest feelings in the world to feel, so sometimes it is easier to pretend you weren't bothered rather than say. 'I respect you do not feel the same way as I do, but this is too painful for me. To see you with other people.'

Don't get me wrong, I was with other people during the years too.

One of them friends with benefits off then on kind of things, but those things never work, and one person always gets hurt at the end from it.

Trust me, I was a nightmare, though, too. Like I said at the beginning, any form of relationship with me would not be a bed of roses. It would be unpredictable, alcohol filled, and a fucking roller coaster from one day to the next. Can you blame people for not wanting to be part of that?

Not really, but in life, you can't just dip in for the good times and then dip out in the bad times.

That person was always me. The wonderful thing about not drinking is I would never in a million years keep calling someone's phone sober.

I am in control of my emotions a lot more, and the difference now is I choose my partner; I do not need him. I don't need anyone to fill a void or fix me. I know I survived the depths of despair; once you survive, that, nothing really fazes you that much.

Of course, I would still feel hurt and pain, but I wouldn't shatter into a million pieces.

It's funny, isn't it, when you see the boys in school who everyone used to think were fit or cool or popular.

You remember those first crushes or how they used to think they were the dogs' bollocks.

It was funny because about six months ago, one of those boys messaged me on Facebook, from school days, clearly on a coke bender. He was on holiday with his Mrs and child. He sent some seedy message in the early hours of the morning, talking about the fun we had as teens.

I was just like 'ewwwe.'

Some people really do not ever change, and they like to think you are still that version of you who would put up with and accept booty calls, let alone booty calls from someone on holiday with his family asleep in the next room.

Sometimes this 35-year-old version of me would love to step back in time and go 'nope, not him.'

Don't waste your tears on any of them, but it's all the years of feeling like shit about myself and getting treated like shit that made me realise in recovery that's not what I want anymore.

It led me to my Darren, the kindest man I've ever known, kind in how he treats my daughter and my dog and how he supports me, and I have someone I can talk to, which means more than anything. He always gives me good advice or tries to help solve problems. He builds me up and doesn't tear me down, and I feel very blessed to have him in our lives.

Back to Ibiza.

Just before I had Isabella, though, I went back over there with my girl group, and it was wild. That week was just incredible. I had pillow box red hair, and we had our week recorded. It was an eighteen-to-thirties week.

I pulled this lad one of the nights, and we jumped over into the marina and snuck into someone's yacht. We got a bit Jiggy, as you do when you are young, drug-fuelled, and horny. We helped ourselves to some drinks, and I even went for a wee in the toilette.

We would have got nicked if we got caught! The next day though, he was on the same booze cruise we were on, so that was a bit embarrassing. I took copious amounts of drugs, though, and soon forgot. What did happen, though, as my friends couldn't wait to tell me the next day, I got my baps out and went up to random girls on the boat, telling them to be free like me.

Then I broke out into the robotic chicken dance with my baps out. The DJ found it so funny he drew attention to it and got the whole boat to do the robotic chicken dance, obvs not as good as my version. I couldn't remember much in fairness, but yea our week got recorded, so we got a DVD of it. Turns out they weren't lying.

I'm so glad things didn't go viral as much then, we went to the Ibiza reunion weekend a few months later, and everyone referred to me as the redheaded chicken girl.

Those kinds of things were fun. I don't regret those things. They were the actions of someone young free, and single.

I never hated myself then. Everyone just thought I was nuts.

I often spent most of my weekends at my friends Jenna's, but we call her Brown because that's her surname.

Brown was in the sixth form then, and we had been on a big session the night before. Brown was like, 'Beth, I have got to do an art project. Is there any chance u will get in a bin bag and I can through the paint at you?' I was like, 'sure, why not'

We got a bit carried away, and Brown jumped over her garden fence and nicked her neighbour's wheelbarrow. She decided to put me in said wheelbarrow and just flick paint at me. We got it all over her garden, and it looked like someone had thrown up an acid tablet all over there.

She had me climbing trees, and all sorts, our other mate Nicole come round in the middle of it like 'what are you two doing?' 'Well, we've robbed the neighbour's wheelbarrow, and Beth said I could flick paint at her for my art project.'

Nicole's like, 'sound can I join in?'

Brown's Mom came back in the middle of it all, and she was fuming. Just at that moment, she was going mad about what we had done to the garden. My dad turned up with KFC for me, which tipped her over the edge.

'My garden's ruined, and now I'm getting southern fried chicken delivered straight to my door.'

(it's a good job she never came around when we made the space cakes because that was trippy).

Sorry, Julie.

Brown has been on lots of adventures with me, she lives in Leeds now, but she is one of my favourite people in the whole world.

You would know when the session would be getting messy because I would be in the resighting kitchen poetry whether people wanted to hear it or not.

At this one party at mine, we were all on MDMA, and we broke the bed jumping off it to see if we could fly. We thought it would be a great idea at the time to fix it with my television holding it up. That was not a good idea. It was a very silly, silly idea.

I remember when I was in the kitchen, though, I read this poem I had written then so, about 13 years ago.

The pigeon people

They call us the pigeon people, much lower than rats
We don't roll with the highflyers and money-grabbing cats
We are what they like to call underpaid working class
But I guarantee when Friday comes, there will be beer in our
glass
We chill with humble expectations happiness will do
Paper in our pockets there will be a hole seeping through
Little things humble us, like a Sunday home-cooked roast
Or if we are stoned, we will chill with cheese on toast
We hit the little locals as soon as it gets dark
We have the odd designer garment (although it's mostly from
Primark)
I love the sweet taste of cigarettes poisoning my tongue
The smoke entering my mouth darkening my lungs
Work I'll admit it is quite dismal if I holiday it will be in Spain
I chat shit (normally moaning about English summer rain)
I take drugs just to entertain my boredom. It usually does the
trick
Just because I'm in casual attire do not presume that I am thick
I used to want to aim for the stars, but now surviving with a tot
or two will do
I may be a pigeon person, and I'll never be noticed by you
We get louder on white powder. Yes, we know that it is mixed
But the rich unloving cats are nothing but money-grabbing
pricks
Our purse strings get tighter with this horrid credit crunch
And gone is your Tenna on a standard Monday lunch
But I'm just a chilled-out creature with a little passion in my
soul
And I'll admit I don't hide this dormant rhyming goal
But if I am a pigeon person, what does that make you?
A tosser in a suit who just hasn't got a clue

I wrote the next poem about a well-known place in Birmingham's town centre people used to end up in after clubbing. If you are a Brummie, I am sure you will relate.

Old SKOOL RAVIN

Did you ever enter the tunnel of doom?
That smelt like poppers in every room
Ten pounds In and ten free drinks
Where there were Indie vibes and overflowing sinks
Or the old church they changed to the Que club
That was a raver maze, a safe hub
With flashing lights, music from cream
Neon lights a raver's dream
Did you wobble into the rainbow when they did wobble on the beach?
Where the toilets needed serious bleach
But the venue was Euphoric, and you were young and ready to Rave
Were you up in arms when they locked things down, those nights you wanted to save?
Did you round your weekend off in Masons with a cheeky Vimto or two?
Because you were winding down from the raving but still had some partying to do
Did you spend Sundays planning your excuses for what you could say to work?
Although you were young and foolish, you knew Monday was going to hurt
Did you go to rave in moon lounge and fall down those winding stairs?
Do you cringe when u look at photos of the style of your hair?
Were you all about the music and connecting with your friends?
Are you sad that you grew up and these days came to an end?
Weren't really into Broad Street because you had to pay on every door
You had budgeted 20 pounds so you couldn't spend more
Did you go to drum and base raves at that death trap they called AIR?

With the crushed cars used as fences and the outside fare
Can you remember the buzz of getting ready before the taxi
came?
Do you miss the days of giving it large now you chill in pjs and
feel lame?
Did you go to go to sleep with the speaker still vibrating in your
head
Did you round your night off with cheesy chips from the legend
Mr. EGG

I went to lots of these places with my girl group. Most of them have little families of their own now. Carly, Nessa, Kate, Laura, Amanda, Caroline, Jenna, and a girl we used to hang around with called Jenny.

These are the Girls I have gone on Holiday with and spent many, many nights out with. There is also the twins Nicole, as I mentioned before, and Kylie and Kezza B who we spent a lot of our youth with. There really are far too many people we hung around with to mention individually, but we really did enjoy our youth.

The craziness is we even threw a Beth is going to rehab party before I went in one big last bender. I sold it to myself, but it then took another six weeks for rehab to happen, so that bender lasted six weeks pretty much.

I will never ever forget the people who have been there throughout the years, and in fairness, I had lived a life so full of fun before it got bad that I have no fear of missing out.

I've Done Ibiza and Amsterdam, and we started raving well before we were old enough too. The thought of going out at night now past ten makes me feel tired, and I haven't worn heels for years; I just can't be arsed.

They make the day feel so much longer, they are uncomfortable, and I went out every weekend from Thursday to Sunday in them for a lot of years.

One of my favourite memories is Carly and Kate's Nans retirement party. We all went there on Es I went as the Angel of Beth instead of the angel of death. We were all in fancy dress tripping out our heads. We went back to Mannor house lane where we had many a party over the years, we were in a Kitchen with Amy Wine House, Bambam from the flintstones, A school Girl, a gangster, two girl ravers, Tinker Belle, Marge Simpson, and Minnie the Mouse, Hen went as Bugs Bunny an all was bloody hilarious. Fancy dress parties on Es are so bloody trippy. Weren't like it was a rave, it was a bloody retirement party.

I have made many memories, too many to even contemplate trying to write down. Here are some poems that may help fill you in the picture.

185

Over The Park with Friends

It all started the very first time I got a feeling of synthetic
happiness
A clear substance that took away my consciousness
Eventually, it took from my core and everything in it
Ironically, the white spirit took my spirit
Where it all started was over park with friends
A simple solution, a means to an end
Oblivion of sorts
That twists up your mind, whispers, and distorts
That's not where it all started, though. There were years of
promiscuousness
A substance simple in the form that, for a while, took away all
loneliness
Until it made me lonelier than I thought it was possible to be
The people I loved were within reach somehow, but left was
only this bottle and Me
Or would it of sounded better if I said the bottle and I
It began in the park, then the pubs and the clubs, then just me
and this bottle, just wanting to die
The first time I drank it, I was transformed
Like a lost little lamb being reborn
But I didn't. Baa I roared
One bottle wasn't enough. I wanted more I was bored
I didn't want to feel anything of anything, and where it all
started made me numb
It was the reason for all my troubles I needed, like fingers need
a thumb
I needed every inch and ounce of it, even the dribbles in the cap
There wasn't enough of it. I could have just lay back, drank
from an ever-pouring tap
Still, I'd want to have the dregs in the pipes
The giver of joy, the fuel for the fights
It started in jest, so I thought
They call me an alcoholic; that's what the big books taught
I'm not just an alcoholic though; I'm much more than that
I can be addicted to people and places as long as they make me
feel crap

186

I can be addicted to feeling low, and I don't know what to do
with the highs
It's very rare now that you would see me cry
I am stone-like in some ways but weak in others
This poem goes out to all the grieving Mothers
I'm sorry for the loss you feel. I'm sure it runs really deep
You won't find it here, though, if answers are what you seek
Because where it all started was pure euphoria; that's how it
drags you in
Then all of a sudden, you're in a war with yourself; you cannot
win
Someone's hijacked your brain cells, someone has over rid your
thoughts
Someone's crushed your dreams you're in the next rehabs
cohorts
You may be institutionalised or put into place for the madness
of the mind
You may be searching endlessly for the euphoria of the first sip,
but it's something you will not find
You will never get it again, no matter how many times you
chase it
You may be given a fruitful world, but with every sip, you
choose to waste it
Chasing the moment where it all began, the transformation
from weak to wild
The glue that built the broken pieces of trauma as a child
The very thing that saved you from the feelings in yourself
Will put you in an urn my friend placed upon your mother's
shelf
So, if you keep on chasing where it started that first hit that first
high
You'll be on the road to nowhere, friend; upon the path, you
may well die
It started at the park with friends
A simple solution, a means to an End

Back A Day

When I was a youth, sausage rolls at Greggs which used to be
Braggs used to be 27p
Which is a good job really because my lunch money
Had a different destiny
It was to go into a pot of 3 pounds 33
3 Ways on a weed or to pay off last week's sub
Then we had to get the rizla and fags to go with our bud
We wore Cabrini tops that felt like we were getting strangled by
the giant hood
We would camp out on sneaky adventures at earls wood woods
When I was a youth, I went to cockshut hill
I think I was around 15 when I tried my first pill
Adventures and havoc, we sure had our fill
Didn't realise these antics would lead me to get so ill
But anyhow, at the time, it was all fun and games
Hiding under subways when it poured, and it rained
Friends for life at that school is what I sure gained
The wagged school parties we had when the neighbours
complained
We lived in a different time a tracksuit bubble
Where the Rockport's on your feet always lead you to trouble
We would chill in loading bays and blend in like the rubble
Getting a stranger to buy our booze was our biggest struggle
If only I had known, then what I do now
Would I have knuckled down more? I don't think so somehow
Because when you are young, you think you know best
Haven't done your homework wagged school on the test
You can't think beyond your Friday night
And you thrive off the drama of a playground school fight
Spent most of my school days put in inclusion
I was probably so stoned it caused me confusion
I loved bopping around in my tracksuit to drum and bass
Boom blaster over the park getting off my face
I look back now, and it fills my heart with pure fear
Belle, you are not leaving this house. Oh no sorry my dear
Because I cannot imagine my baby doing those things

But I suppose her hands wouldn't be bounded by sovereign
rings
Or gold necklaces and hoop earrings that weigh down your ears
Oh, don't do what your Mommy did would be one of my
biggest fears

When I think back to some of our nights out, I think of the Kings of Leon. Playing that song, 'your sex is on fire.'

I think of the excitement during the pre-drinks and the conversations in the week about what we would be wearing or discussing the gossip from the week before.

It was exciting. Looking back, though, I would outstay my welcome at some of the sessions that were on the weekend. I would always be staying at different friends' houses.

The girl Jenny I mentioned earlier I stayed at a lot, and I want to say. Although, we lost contact, I am eternally grateful for that.

They still lived with their parents, but I lived alone in my flat, which was far from where we all grew up.

They had to pass their parents a bit of housekeeping, but I had to keep a home running, and that flat that was party central on the weekend could be a tad lonely in the week.

I did love it though it gave me independence and responsibility. My priorities were muddled, though, a nineteen-year-old choosing between paying the full rent or taking out the weekend spending money.

This following poem is written about a night we had at an old, converted church in Birmingham's town centre.

I had blonde pixy style hair, one of those haircuts that you look back on and think was I auditioning as an extra in lord of the rings. My eyes bulged like Smeagol sometimes, and I would probably look at the drugs in my hand like, 'hello, my precious.'

This night out was before I ever experienced Ibiza, and it blew my mind.

What a Night in The Q club

It was like some fucked up, but delightful dream

Felt like I was walking on clouds, walking through the hallways
in cream

Shot birds in pink netted skirts light luminous green

And if that was a little taste of Ibiza, then fucking ell I liked
what I seen

Felt the need to triple-drop just because I could

Nothing like what I felt dancing in the Q club

Couldn't stop smiling room full of love

Hardcore ravers no room for bud

My blue eyes were now black as the pupil took over

Drinking water, far from soba

Glow sticks, rave paint, black glasses with white rims.

People communicating through wide eyes and swinging grins

Heart-pounding music a little hardcore

Satisfied with the amounts I'd taken no need to take more

I'd made the correct decision to wear flats, so my feet weren't
sore

The next morning my gums were sweet as well, and so was my jaw

Faces in the crowd you recognise, but you won't stop if you start to chat

And out of those amazing hours, I only smoked a few fags out of my pack

Needed to soak up every second of this night. I will never forget

I never fell over or chatted too much like a drunken wreck

I loved every second of it. The next morning never even had a come down

I just chilled; even ate felt pretty sound

In my own little world, in cream although people were around

Got no rhythm to dance, so I just jumped up and down

It wasn't like I was drunk every think being a haze

And that place was like a huge bubble, a maze

But that might have been cause of the class A's

Didn't think it was going to be that good. I was actually amazed

The hottest thing is it used to be a church

You stand there amazed as your eyes search

You go dancing, not get chatted up by rugged Geza's that try to flirt

There were men in white jump suits and a man who refused to put on his shirt

Every once was entertaining

Some of the men in there were hot, to be fair, so I was not complaining

But as the light seeped in through the window

I knew it was time for me to go

I loved it can't wait for the real thing

Next time I'm wearing acid colours and bright pink angel wings

The colours the people everything so bright

Go to cream trust it will be the best night of your life!

Do you want to hear something ironic?

At the time, I worked in some offices by the mailbox in town, and next door to our offices was the paper printing offices, the Mail and Sun.

I got asked last minute if I wanted to be in an article because the person who was supposed to do it had pulled out.

I was like, 'yea, go on then, sure,' I had to pose with my arms folded. I had a beige Wholly hat on.

The article's title was 'I deserve a cheap drink at the end of the week'.

It was about alcohol culture and the places that did cheap alcohol or ten pounds in ten free drinks kind of deals.

You would never get that these days.

I did a whole article on why I thought alcohol prices should be low so that young people could go out and have fun.

The opposite column was a girl in boxing gear who was anti-booze.

I went to the pub that Friday night and the lads were reading copies of it, and everyone was laughing. I thought I was well cool.

I'm not embarrassed by it because that was my way of thinking at the time. It is the way of thinking for most young people. I find it ironic now that I'm writing a book on alcoholism.

I use this next poem in schools when I do my drug and alcohol awareness workshops.

I clearly wrote it on a comedown, but I ask the young people to find the dangers and consequences in the poem.

Consequences

Is it me, or does anyone else feel weird the buzz isn't quite the
same as last week
As I rub my thighs up and down as I quickly speak
Is it me, or does anyone else feel like time has just whizzed past
What have we done for the last 4 hours? How long does this
weird feeling last

Have a little want some more, pure greed
As I blow my nose, realise I'm having a nosebleed
How embarrassing I'm going to like a right lightweight
Please move that curry-filled plate

Quite hungry, but I don't think I will ever eat again
My stomach is in knots through up the water I just drank, oh
I'm in pain
8.00 clock in the morning and were searching for dribbles of
tots like bagheads
Feaning for nicotine, such fag heads

The shakes are kicking in. An hour ago, I was boiling, almost
sweating
I must have repeated myself a hundred times, kept forgetting
My eyes bright red eyeballs diluted
Lungs polluted

Thought that this shit was meant to keep u on the level
What level?
The level when we all chat shit
Tell people we hate that we love them, and we can't sit

I'm not saying never again because I'll probably be in the same
state next week,
You work all week, why not have fun? Don't make life feel
bleak
It's just on Sunday, I looked like an advertisement for why not
to drink
As I had my head rested by the sink

Eyes so heavy, hurt to blink
And you think I wonder what everyone else thinks
What did I do? What did I say? Who did I slag off?
How on earth did I rip my new favourite top

I need sleep, can't eat, can't sleep. It's the day
Light seeps through the window as you're crazy night slips
away
And on the night when you were right, you thought you were
having the best time ever
The next day you say I'm not doing that again nah never

Depends on who you are around. I suppose sometimes it good
depends on the atmosphere
It's well to deer
And probably mixed
Numbs ya lips
Takes pounds off your hips
anyway, who's up for their next fix

When I was searching for some relevant poems to put into this section, I was excited to put in all the fun I had. Then I came across this poem I had written as a teenager. It saddened me more than most of the other poems I have written.

I was sad for the younger version of myself.
The version of myself that let people treat me this way.
(Booty call Beth.)
The girl who was always the drunkest and easiest.
I just wanted to be loved, for someone to see that's not who I was, but alcohol and drugs make you do strange things.
Act in strange ways and become promiscuous and easy.

Drugs really didn't agree with me. The comedowns took me to some very dark places, so I stopped them and committed my time and dedication to being a full-blown alcoholic instead, (loyalty and all that.)

I read this poem, and I just thought, today, I am going to be kind to myself.

Reading these things makes me want to be all the more successful, as a thank you to the younger, naive version of myself that got me to this point.

I cannot go back in time and hug the younger version of myself, but the person I am today can aspire to blow all those feelings out of the water and lay the foundations for the older version of myself to look back on and be proud.

I am still proud of the promiscuous little pisshead I used to be because I needed that to survive at the time.

It has made me strong, and hopefully, those internal battles I had are going to help other people see they are not the only ones who have made mistakes.

I appreciate Darren so much more because of the way I was treated in the past or the way I acted. I would never ever want to hurt him; he wouldn't want to intentionally hurt me. I could never imagine us being in that horrible game of chess with each other of tit for tat. Our relationship has made me grow as a person and it is not co dependant in anyway. A level of love I'd never known. It doesn't suffocate me, or hurt me, or consume me, it's just well, nice, happy, funny, kind, connection, communication, conversations, encouragement and loyalty.

I Lay Back

I lay back. I was scared, but it did not show at least, I don't
think it showed on my face
He kept kissing me, and beer, and fags were all I could taste
He'd been going on at me for weeks. When he was drunk, he
would beg, and he would plead
He put one hand up my skirt with the other he, stroked my hair,
and said, 'you are the one girl I need
I was shaking. He was that drunk he didn't notice
He lit up a half-smoked joint put it towards my lips said 'smoke
this.'
He looked straight into my blue eyes with his blue eyes. He just
looked at me for a while. Neither of us moved
He couldn't tell I was nervous as his hand slowly moved
I wasn't nervous because I was a virgin
It was because I'd always been in love with him
He'd never noticed me before
I said, 'you won't use me, will you? Because, well, you know I
like you, and then I stopped myself from saying those words'
He just looked at me, pulled up my skirt, smiled, then kissed
me. I guess that was easier for him
He put his body into my body slowly at first, and then he turned
his head away from me and started going in and out of me quite
fast
I Thought how long the moment in time will last
I guess I knew what I was letting myself in, for he was like a
drug to me I always needed a next fix
I knew all he wanted to do was use me, but I was hypnotised by
his lips
As the feelings started rushing through my body, you know, the
ones I mean I scream, 'I love you'
He pretended he did not hear, then he unconvincingly said it
back
he carried on for 10 minutes or so, and then, well that was that
I phoned him, but he didn't answer, and he called me one
Friday late. I knew exactly what he was ringing me for
I lay back, nervous he couldn't tell I was nervous, and every
Friday, I went back for more

Now this book is entitled through Isabella's eyes, the thought of my little girl writing down those words would break me into a million pieces, and I'm sure it's not an easy read, some of the parts anyway to those who love me.

Remember the part, when I said our failures or the things, we consider to be failures are not failures if we learn from them.

Well, I'm hoping that's the case with my beautiful Belle. Hopefully, she will get all the beautiful parts of life because I can protect her from those darker bits, because I know what it feels like.

I can look at her and think if I pick up that bottle again, I'll take my eye off the ball. I'll be so consumed by my own pain she will be craving attention from the wrong type of people.

That's reason enough for me not to want to drink again. I never knew another way before, but now I do, and it would be a choice. No matter what drove me to it, I'd be aware of the consequence.

I'm not willing to make my Belle pay that price. What I'd like to drink is her giggles, bottled up in a jar, or any tears she may cry, so she doesn't have to.

That's not possible, though, but now I see the world with a clear view. Not only have I seen the beauty in it, but I've seen the evil in it too. I'm less naive because I am awake. I see all the people who played me like a fiddle and all the people who disappeared when I was no longer the evening laughingstock.

So, while she still has beautiful pure, naive eyes, I don't want to corrupt her view. I'll just be her eyes for her for a little while, in the hope she never has to see some of the things that my eyes seen.

I finished that song, by the way, the one we used to sing over the park.

Ten years on ended up in rehab
I took the same drugs and drink, she and he had
Just my brain is wired a different way
No longer fun and games I don't want to play
I just took them in fun and jest
Now my whole worlds a crumbling mess
It's not all right...

So, on conclusion, what can we do to help ourselves.

Oh, wow, I did not think this part would feel so emotional. I don't want to leave you now feel like we were just getting somewhere.

The first step, of course, is acknowledging we have a problem. That's the most challenging part; some people will live their entire lives in denial. Suppose you are reading this and still in denial or toying with drinking. In that case, the likelihood is you may have a few relapses ahead, but that's ok because, hopefully, you will learn from them.

There is no harm, even if you are in active addiction dipping your toes in the water and seeing what recovery is all about.

You never know; something may click. The most important thing is you build a foundation of the recovering community around you.

I did write this part when I first wrote the book, and since then, I have realised that only some have the best intentions.

I wanted to save the world at one point, and I still do, but now from the safety of my laptop, I hope someone will connect with the words though and it will help.

Watching people at the front-line relapse has been too painful because I have felt their pain as if it were my own.

People have exploited my kindness and twisted me up in knots, but I'm not so eager now to see the good in everyone.

That sounds negative, doesn't it?

Don't get me wrong, this world has some beautiful souls. I know a few, and I know a few ladies in recovery have my back as I have theirs.

There have been some wonderful friends that have supported me, even though they have had their own battles to deal with (Stacie and Jen pen, I love you, my girls, always had my back, haven't you girls, made some of those telesales jobs more fun,)

The first time I met Jen, I was wearing my Nanny Wins Knickers because I had, had a shower at hers and never took any with me. They were literally big granny pants. I had rolled over about five times. I flashed them to her on our fag break and was

200

like, look, 'I'm wearing me nans pants.' We instantly became friends from there.

Stacie is a whirlwind of creativity with fiery red hair and a beautiful, unique singing voice.

What I mean by not seeing the good in everyone is that old saying as you get older, you get wiser. Remember I said I had the mind of a 15-year-old going in, so I've been sober three years, so in a way, I guess I still have a teenage mind, just a less pissed one.

Good people in recovery, though, are like gold dust. There will be no judgment if you fall.

We make the mistake of trying to do things on our own.

To get back to work, education being parents, but like overcompensating parents, the daily grind, and we feel that if we are ticking the boxes of what society seems to class as functioning individuals, we cannot be doing so bad.

I always say the first thing people ask you when you say you have a partner is, 'how long have you been together?'

Like you win a prize the longer you have been with someone.

They never ask, 'are you happy? How does he/she treat you?'

It goes back to the two point-four children, a land rover, and the same meal every Tuesday kind of scenario.

Going to meetings or recovery groups, joining Facebook groups, and reading books (hopefully this one) takes up time in our busy lives. However, doing things on our own can be lonely.

Even if we are surrounded by people who love us like family and friends, unless they have experienced the feelings of addiction, as hard as they may try (and they do try) they can't really understand, and how can we expect them too really.

I see the odd eye roll like, 'Surely, she should be over it by now, for God's sake, she can't drink booze anymore; get over it, will ya.'

No! I will never get over it, I will learn to live with it and use that pain to fuel my success, but I have to work hard every single day to not press the FUCK IT button.

Talking to people that genuinely understand is like free therapy, one addict helping another.

That's what this book is supposed to be about, really.

If it sells only one and helps that person, it has done what it was intended to do.

If it sells millions, just think of all the amazing face creams I could buy.

My skin will glow like those worms. I may even glow in the dark. Who knows.

There are no data charts in this book or scientific research behind it. Well, that's a bit of a lie because I learned things about the addictive brain etc, so it's not all just pure waffle.

This book lists a few things that have helped me that, in turn, may help you.

That's how I rate success, not big cheques in the bank.

There is nothing more beautiful than seeing someone turn their life around.

We talked about visual things like calendars and tick lists, (Thanks Tom, if you want me to return the favour by being in any kissing scenes, let me know, sorry Darren, I love you aha)

Darren's not jealous; he is as chilled as a cucumber.

Routines are key. Talking of Darren, he takes the mick out of me because He can tell when I'm getting tired and grumpy, but I'll openly admit it. I bloody love my sleep, my dreams, and whatever craziness my mind creates.

We talked about learning from our mistakes and not being defined by them.

In life, humour can go such a long way. Not taking life too seriously, you could say to someone, the skies are lovely and blue today. They will respond with something like, 'yea, well makes a change, probably rain in a bit,' fun sponge, aha.

Being able to laugh at yourself, not in a derogatory way, but I can take Banta, I can laugh at myself, and I can even laugh at some of the craziness I did in addiction, like vacuuming up a puddle of water or someone telling me if I put my phone battery in the microwave it would charge it, it did not by the way obvs.

I laugh at some of the bad situations I got myself in and think, what the actual fuck, how did I survive that week in and week out?

There was a drama week in, and week out. That's why I love my peace so much now. It's quite freeing, laughing at the things that hurt you or looking back at your ex's like yep, that was breakdown number one. That was breakdown number three aha.

I'm just saying that in jest, I don't wish anyone any ill feelings, life's too short. Thanks for inspiring me to write this book, but don't ask me for any royalty cheques you can piss right off. They are for my Belles.

It may be too raw for you to dig deep, or you might just not be the kind of person who can take the piss out of themselves. Just try not to get consumed by negative thoughts.

I know I'm not perfect. I know I'm loud and brash at times, I butt in when I'm excited in conversations, I am impulsive, and I can be moody when I'm tired, hungry, or hormonal.

I get fixations and obsessions on hair dye, trainers, or the latest health fad.

I go on about recovery a lot. I bring the conversation back to experiences I may have had. The list goes on.

I'm dyslexic, and my grammar is appalling. I don't know my left and right, you may have guessed by now I swear a lot too.

But I also know I am kind. I truly would help anyone in need, I'm loyal, and if I love you, I love you with all my heart. I will go out of my way to help strangers, and I am trying to silence this disease of the mind every single day. I'd go to the ends of the earth, walk on hot coals, and gargle glass for my Belle, and none of that would compare to how hard giving up the drink was. But right now, I am sober, and that's good enough for me.

You could try new hobbies, try to find out who you really are. Trying new things can give you a new lease of life, and I can open up doors for you socially and maybe even careerwise.

It could be anything; maybe you've always wanted to learn to cook. What harm can there be in learning a new skill that would enhance your life?

On that note, we can go on to something else. We talked about the big one that plays a factor in everything.

Fear

We spoke about how the fear of success can be scarier than the fear of failing, but please try to push on through. If I had given in to my fear, I wouldn't have achieved some of the wonderful things I have since been in recovery.

The wonderful things that you can achieve too.

Including writing the pages of this book and getting all the stuff out of my head and onto paper, in the hope that it may help others to feel a little comfort in its pages.

The past mistakes and how they do not define the person we are today.

We can reinvent ourselves as often as we need to until we truly discover who we are.

That doesn't mean to say all the different people we have been along the way were fake. It just means it was trial and error, and that was the person we thought we were at the time.

I think differently, and I act differently now. I even dress a bit differently, (I don't flash my baps anymore).

My brother Henry says that all the different outfits I wear are for my multiple personalities.

He also says some of my trainers make me look like a fifteen-year-old skater girl.

I give as good as I get, though, and it's all just said in jest. Maybe he wishes deep down he was a fifteen-year-old skater girl. 'Don't worry, Hen, I won't judge if you come round mine dressed as Avril Lavigne.'

In a way, that is true. Some days I want to feel like a badass bitch. Wednesday, I feel like a bit of a chav. Sometimes I'm a hippy and Zen. Friday I might want to get a bit dolled up, put loads of makeup on, and do all my hair. I might want to chill in my pyjamas.

I do a lot less of that now, though. Before, I always used to have my baps out because I thought that that was my best feature. If I had a low-cut top on, that would draw attention to them, and then people wouldn't necessarily be able to see what was happening in my head or the pain in my eyes.

From the outside, it may have looked like I was oozing confidence and proudly showing them off as it's for the world to see. Actually, it was the opposite. Dressing like that came from a place of insecurity. I've attracted the wrong type of men and put myself out there as an object rather than my own person with thoughts and feelings.

Do I regret dressing like that?

No, because it was a defence mechanism that served me well for quite a while.

Just like I don't regret my addiction for the same reasons.

I mean, I don't dress like a nun now by all means and probably do the same thing with my hair extensions, I have all different colours, depending on how I feel on that day.

To look like I'm confident when I am breaking it inside, I put my red ones in a curl all my hair because that makes me feel confident.

I'm not telling you all to start dyeing your hair every other day, but anything that works for you, if it works, then great.

A lucky Charm, a certain style, a smell of perfume or Cologne.

They're all things that make us who we are.

If that changes over the years or if you grow out of looking a certain way because it doesn't fit with the today version of you.

Then dress however the hell you want and express yourself through it I'll make some slogan tops, 'Fuck the System.' or something.

We talked about triggers, figuring out what they are, who they are, and how to avoid them.

Believe me, this gets easier with time. As we said previously, your ability to set healthy boundaries will grow and happen naturally.

Procrastination we all do it from time to time. I did it with this book, but identifying why we do it on the essential things is a good way of understanding where we are sometimes. We just simply need to give ourselves a kick up our own arses.

Sometimes things will happen when they're meant to happen.

Changing the mindset of negatives into positives.

I'm not going to lie to you and tell you every day and recovery is going to be fucking fantastic because that's unrealistic, and it simply is not. What I will say to you, though...

Your darkest days in recovery will never be as dark and all-consuming as your days in active addiction.

Learning to sit in your pain, process it, work through it, and figure out solutions is powerful.

What do we learn from masking pain with alcohol or drugs?

Nothing. alcohol is a depressant, so it may, just strangely enough, amplify those feelings.

It gives us an extraordinary instant couple of seconds of remarkable gratification, but then instantly follows your problems, multiplying tenfold.

So instead of working together with yourself to become a stronger, better version, you literally became your own worst enemy.

That internal battle of the mind takes all your energy up, so you simply have no time for positivity, or to work on figuring your way out through your pain.

You are too busy running from it, chasing the next 5 seconds of bliss, your fix will give you until the five seconds don't exist anymore.

But you're still doing it in the hope that maybe, just maybe, you may find peace again.

You will never find peace from something that breaks you or numbs you. Once a cucumber turns into a pickle, it can never be a cucumber again. You will always be chasing the old days regurgitating memories in kitchens talking about the good old days. While actually just being stuck in the mud, recycling the same stories week in week out.

Drinking dreams are shit. Trust me, I know.

But talk about them. It takes power out of them.

Just like those sneaky little addictive voices, we get in our minds, waiting for the chink in our armour to strike.

Toxic people and relationships, if you can be happy alone, you are more likely to succeed in a relationship. If you seek a relationship to fill a void, then you are just doing the same thing you did with drink or drugs.

No human wants to be lonely. I get that, I've always loved the thought of being in love, but that's just it.

Are we in love with our partner at the time? Or just the thought of it, the fairy-tale side, the social media relationship update side.

I keep these kinds of things private now, I've never been one to put stuff like that on Facebook, but that's more because my previous relationships were so unpredictable my status would have changed every other week.

The most important thing I would want you to take from this book (is not that you can get jobs on Gumtree throwing custard over men for 50 pounds)

But the part where I said about forgiveness and forgiving yourself.

As if this version of you now is stepping back in time and giving the broken version of you a hug.

The child version of you, that will help to heal your inner child.

Forgive yourself and change your mindset from victim to warrior.

When I was in rehab, the group of people I was with in there we called ourselves the warriors.

In the four weeks, I became closer to these people than I had been to people I had known all my life.

One of them died shortly after, which was really sad as she was trying so hard to remain sober. She was sober when she passed, though.

Actually, a few people I knew from where I went to rehab have passed away, which is heart-breaking.

We showed each other the maskless, broken vulnerable versions. Of each other, and that did not scare us away from each other.

So, it made me realise I didn't always have to hide behind the front.

Because people like you more when you're honest, and if they still don't like you when you are being true to who you really are, then they can quite simply just fuck off.

Wish them well and all the best, and I can get there way, and you can go your way, no Fucks given.

If you don't know who you are right now and feel overwhelmed, I will list all the places you can think of where you can go for help.

Thank you from the bottom of my heart for taking the time to read this book, and I hope even just one thing helped you. I wish you lots of love on your journey and hope you find peace.

I did not get to this point in my life on my own. I have worked very hard to maintain my recovery, but the people who loved me when I couldn't find it in me to love myself. I see you, acknowledge you, and forever will be grateful to you.

Whether that be my best friends from childhood or my old neighbours when I was at rock bottom (one of them took me to rehab, thank you Tracy, for everything)

My family, the rehab centres, and the strangers who I've met along the way.

My previous boss Jula, who showed me tough love, but it was love because she knew underneath it all I was a good person, as is she.

She went above and beyond for me and holds a very special place in my heart.

Michelle, who sadly passed away but also worked at St Basil's, she saw something in me, encouraged me, and would help anyone. She was a pocket rocket and would light up a room. I hope you're having fun up in heaven.

My friend Bonnie, whom I worked with, gave me compassion, and went out of his way to help me find the light.

My beautiful daughter, the light of my life and the reason for my existence, you, my darling, are all that is good in this world.

Darren, for sitting there endless nights watching me tap away, believing in me and encouraging me.

My guardian angels, thank you for all the signs you have given to me, I see them all, they have healed me, and I know that death is not the end now, it is only just the beginning, while I am on this earth though I may as well make the most of it ay.

To my close family, I put you through pain I am sorry. Thank you for not giving up.

I am so proud of all of you. My Nan would just be so proud of you Dad you had a dream and you have made it come true. She would of adored Carter Charlie and what a wonderful father you are. Hen, she would have seen what a wonderful man you have turned out to be.

My older Brothers you are doing so well made such big waves on the music scene and made me an auntie to Kendal and Blake my gorgeous niece and nephew.

Mom, I'm sure Jackie is looking after Mollie, light a candle when you feel lost it will guide you.

To my friends who have sadly passed away, I will continue to speak your name, so your legacy lives on. I wish that was not the case but unfortunately that is something beyond my control. What I do have though is a voice that I can use to create better mental health services, addiction services and social services. I will use your angel wings as inspiration to ruffle some feathers. I'll look out for your signs.

I dedicate this book to all of you, but most importantly, I dedicate this book to my Aunty Jeanette. You were a shining star on my dark nights. A beacon of hope. That is why I named one after you. When I was broken, so very broken, you put me back together piece by piece. I will never ever forget how you loved me when I did not love myself.

I was at a crossroads, I had one foot over the cliff and nearly went over the edge.

Not only did your love and support help me, but in turn, hopefully, it will help others. I know this has changed how my daughter will grow up and her perspective of the world now.

You will never know how much your love saved me; I love you, I loved you when I was a child, a teenager an adult and I will always love you. You have always been there unconditionally and that is what love is, I know that now.

I will leave this book with a few poems about my Belle, some other relevant poems ending on the Final Poem.

Mother

I was born, I was raised I'm trying to raise another
No one gives you a qualification or a certificate for being a
mother
However, every day I see her eyes, I see the turning of her mind
I see her sharing and cuddling with a heart that is kind
My girl would never bully another. She would not dare
She tells her mommy off if I forget myself and swear
My princes wouldn't litter. She has shouted at a kid to put it in
the bin
She was half his size, but I kind of felt for him
She sings songs in the bath and splashes around in the water
My Angel loves to rhyme her words; you can tell she's, my
daughter.
Ohhh, she has a temper just like mine!!
Slamming her door in my face; this girl is only five. Can we
pause time?
When she is 13, I don't want her to make the mistakes I did
She will look at me like I am old, like I don't know how it is to
be a kid
How do I tell her mommy took drugs n mommy drank quite a
bit?
In fact, my daughter of mine mommy was quite a little shit
Please do not do what I did to my guides
It's just life, not a destiny child's film. We are all survivors
I'm trying to guide you, trying to love you. I'm not your
opponent
I cuddle you in bed and read your stories, wishing I could just
freeze that moment
You will grow older, and everything I do
It will annoy you!!!!!!
You will not want to do your homework
I pray with all my heart it goes out of fashion to twerk
You are and always will be.
The best thing that ever happened to me
You drive me bonkers. Do my head right in
Within my heart is where you will always live in

My Child's Eyes

My child's eyes.
Cannot tell any lies
I can see straight through
The dopey, the white, and the perfectly blue
She is all that I wholeheartedly live for
My happiness, my insanity but all that I adore
She is genuinely a good girl with a heart pure and kind
My blue pearl in the ocean, the rarest of find
I wake up. I kiss her
She goes to school. I miss her
She tells me about her day
I say did you have hot dinners she says only on Friday
She likes the fish finger peas and mash
I rewind to the ice cream scoop. I don't even want to ask
She was the star of the week
My creative wonderful mathematical geek
She likes Math
Who on the planet likes Maths??
Algebra, or however you spell it
Have any of you adult humans ever used it?
Didn't think so
The moral of my poem was I adore this child though
She brings me white feathers she finds and says that's you're
Nanny Win
She can't really remember her, but I think she feels her deep
within
When I was pregnant with this bundle of pure and utter hope
My Nanny Win would laugh at me, wondered how my dad
would cope
With loving something so precious as what she is to everyone
The shimmer of a rising moon, the light of a dawning sun
To all of us, you are everything, my child can you tell
My naughty child Isabella, every other day, it's Bell
Forever will I love you until my dying Breath
Next time you write my Mother's Day card, you best sign it
mommy and not Beth

My Little Lady

My little lady is growing up, has her own little style
She's getting little bud cups, but I'm still in denial
We bicker at times well, most days, actually
Only for a bit, then she's back to being my bestie
It's normally in the mornings about brushing her hair
I'm like, 'just go to school like a tramp then, Belle I really don't
care
But I do, it's beautiful I want her to look after it and wear it
with pride
So, I grab the brush when she's not looking and start brushing
like, 'ahhhh I lied.'
She's hilarious, burns me all day long, shouts in the street, My
Mom wears hair extensions
So, I pretend to call the teacher and request a detention
The thing is, we are very similar, so we are going to but heads
It took me a long time to get her back to sleeping in her own
bed
But I need that bit of space to reflect and unwind
Before morning comes and she starts to whine
About utter nonsense, but I suppose that's what kids do
Clean your teeth, brush your hair, for god's sake, where is your
other shoe
By the time we are walking down, though, we are fine
Although every minute she's like, Mom, what's the time
So, I get annoyed and blag her she's late
Caliche, I know, but she's my little best mate
She said the other day, she got overwhelmed at school, and it
brought her to tears
As a parent, those things are up there with our fears
She doesn't cry that often, so when she does, I know it must be
bad
The thought of her being in school without me, tears rolling,
made me so sad
But she is strong, my Belle is, and we wind each other up rotten
By the time she was at the youth centre playing with the other
kids, those tears were forgotten
That's what I love getting to take her to work with me

My sidekick, my, baby, my MINI Me
She's clever, she's kind, she is sassy
Got a Bridgnorth accent and now thinks she's classy
She is growing up but will always be my baby
I see you through my little LADY

Belsy Bum

I picked her up from school today and noticed her smiling face
I thought today must have been a good day as we exited the
place
Walked through the playground, happy to see each other out of
the school gates
She was like, 'do you want to hear the playground drama
Mommy that happened today with my mates?'
I was like 'always,' and she told me about her friend's secret
crushes, and I said, 'Belle have you ever had a Crush?'
She went bright red and was like, 'no, Mommy anyway, just
Shhhh'
I knew then that she had, but she didn't want to tell me, and it
made me sad but giggle a little inside
Where's my baby gone, straight to my face. I could tell it was
the first time she white lied
OH gosh, I remembered the sleepover parties and talks of the
popular boys at that age
Would it be animalistic if, before she turns to a teen, I lock her
in a cage?
Only joking. I wouldn't cage her; I want her to be free like a
bird
Always fly back, though, so I can listen to those words, that
word
'I Love you, Mommy'
'Oh, princess, I love you too, more than you will ever know'
She's only a child, still my baby, but part of me grieves for that
one day she'll go
Off to UNI or traveling or chasing her dreams, of course, I want
that for her always
She healed a broken heart with those four words she says

Insecurity

I wish my daughter could see in herself what I see
At the minute, though, she is full of doubt and insecurity
We can have conversations and talk about worries and fears
We can have cuddles straight after she releases her tears
In general, she's a happy child, but she can be shy and insecure
Most of the time, she acts far more mature.
Than I do
She's like, seriously, I am 9, and I act far more seriously than
you
Today she said a child took the mic out of her because she ran
slow on sports day
I was like Belle are you planning on becoming an Olympic
runner and she was like 'nah no way
So, I was like, you might not be able to run as fast as some of
the other kids
But whatever you do, you always give
100 percent you are going to be better at some things than
others
But I will never be one of those mothers...
That pushes you into doing something you don't want to do
Only do it if it brings joy to you
I bet that kid who said you ran slow can't write stories the same
way that you write
So don't let those words fill your mind at night
You cannot be excellent at everything; that wouldn't be fair
So don't let that person see that you care
Why weren't they focusing on their own race rather than
looking at how you run
It's supposed to be the school sports day. It's just a bit of fun
Concentrate on the things you are good at, and don't worry
about the rest
Next time someone brings you down, at least you know you
tried your best
Or turn round and look them straight in the face
Tell them to concentrate on their own race
Mind their own business worrying about what you do in yours
Cuz Mommy will still be there to greet you with an applause

Silver in the Moon

She is the fire in the sun and the silver of the moon
With an infectious laugh, I wish I could bottle like perfume
Her hug withdraws all my anger. Her touch takes away any pain
Love her button nose, the beautiful sound of her saying her name
Sometimes she stresses me out the love is there always, without any
doubt
The moment she is gone, oh, how I miss her
My heart beats a little faster when I kiss her
I think she is now what makes my heart move
With her silly songs that actually soothe
About how, apparently…. her mommy stinks of poo and wee
She gets her silliness from me
She is everything I could have possibly wished for
Times it by a million and more
Her face is the only face. If I had to pick a face, I'd want to see
It just proves money doesn't buy happiness. I get all of this joy for
free

Cost of Living

I can't stop thinking about the old
Who are going to freeze from the cold
Because they cannot afford to top up their metre
When they do, it gets eaten up by the electric heater
So, they sit there with blankets, don't want to make a fuss or moan
But the cold goes straight through to the bone
Forget the frail
They name it a cost-of-living crisis, so we must prevail
What about the new-born babies who need heat
So, to warm them, the mother simply doesn't eat
Then she has no energy for the night feeds
She's new to this but has to put first the baby's needs
Forget the frail
They name it the cost-of-living crisis, so we must prevail
Then there are the children already in poverty
Showering less gold dust to their bully
Uniform covered in the day's stains
Smelly tramp to add to the names
Yet the parents are struggling to do the weekly shop
Because they upped the prices on the lot
Forget the frail
They name it the cost-of-living crisis so we must prevail
Just got over the covid lockdowns and isolation trauma there
Those CEO's pockets are bulging, so they don't care
Seen advice to have a 4 min shower MAX
You work an extra day to cover the cost, up pipes council tax
Forget the frail
They name it the cost-of-living crisis, so we must prevail
Food banks cannot keep up with the demands
Mothers contemplating only fans
To be seen by the many luring eyes
Wonder if them at the top even believe their own lies
Forget the frail
They name it the cost-of-living crisis, so we must prevail
2022 people getting on ok pushed into poverty
By the way, we are upping mortgage rates come 2023

I cannot stop thinking about the old
With freezing bones sitting in the cold
Or the babies with hungry mothers
Who gets its milk from those human udders
Or the child in poverty who gets bullied at school
My heart bleeds for you all...
But.......
Forget the frail
They name it the cost-of-living crisis, so we must prevail

In The Fear

Through the guilt and the shame, she was paralysed
In the darkness in the shadows, you won't believe that the sun
can Rise
In the cycle, in the fear drowning in an ocean of tears, she cries
If only she could see, she still has a little fire left in those sad
eyes
All it takes is for her to see there is far much more than this
As she opens up the bottle of the devil's kiss
She bottle watches; there's so much that she's missed
The anger she awakes with a cold clenched fist
In the mirror, she cannot bare what she's become
She's a sister, she's a daughter, she is someone's Mom
She is someone who she hates and who she's running from
So, she drinks to forget till the day is done
She is bitter, she's resentful, she was full of dreams
Till she washed them all away, ripped those at the seams
If only I could tell her just how much she means
To the people who love her, she is lost now, or so it seems
There is a fire burning dimly; it just needs to ignite
So, she can remember who she was before she lost this fight
Use the hope that she has to drown out the fear at night
For in this darkness, this deep darkness, there is still some light
They say, stay in your lane
Don't chase the stage; don't wish for the fame
Well, who said the path I was on was my lane anyway, You?
Well, if that's the case, I will double-take times two
Stay in my lane, mind my own business, head down, stay quiet
Well, that starves my soul like a fad crash diet
If I see injustices, I will speak up
Do what I can to lift the weak up
Weak from, carrying the load
Of staying in that lane and sticking to that road
That others said they must travel keeping right on track
Stepping over the lines in the pavement till one day, they all
crack
To release a bubbling volcano, an eruption of the mind

219

Of seeing the irony of hypocrisy by the ones who post pictures
hashtags be kind
Because they are following trends
Luring in new friends
The kind of people who tell you to stay in your lane
As they take shortcuts and hide from the rain
Or piggyback off your ideas
Indulge in the thought of your fears
While they sit back
Chat
Bare shit
The irony of it
Do not tell me to stay in my lane
If that means I lose, and you gain
I've never premeditated about which way I'm going
Others manipulate their path with dark seeds they have been
sowing
I do not need to stay in my lane, and neither do you
And to the people who tell you too
Just a simple nod of the head, a polite fuck you
Will do

Walk With Me

Walk with me, we will plan, or we can reminisce
Walk with me; you shall get through this
For each moment you don't do
The only path that you knew
You take a step further while we walk
We can stride in silence or slowly talk
I see you see the old path calling. It whispers to me too
Some days it screams so loud I wish I could seal my ears with glue
Walk with me; the sounds shall fade
Walk with me; see the steps you've made
New paths will appear while you are walking forward
Some may make you uneasy and socially awkward
It's a learning curve
A bump in the road, a trip up the curb
But keep evolving
You're not hiding from truths. You are problem-solving
Even when you don't feel like it
See your path Walk through it, even take time to sit
In emotions, you run from fears you have
Even the ones that made you mad
Because while there is anger, there Is passion; flip it around
So, you can drown out the old path sound
Walk with me, we will plan, or we can reminisce
Walk with me, you will get through this

FOMO, NO

On route home from Brum last night with a bus smelling like
weed
Watching early clubgoers tucking into kebab stand feeds
On my way to New Street station, fearing the crowds
Of night-time bustles when it's twice as loud
As the daytime commuter trains
With young drunken girls forgetting their own names
Football watchers with jaws swinging in WH Smith
Buying overpriced beer, I questioned
Do I miss this
Is it FOMO?
No
It's fear of not getting home though
There is a reason I keep myself in at night
Because it seeps into my mind when it's in my sight
The flashbacks of nights out, not remembering how I got back
The basic human communication skills I lack
When I would make myself vulnerable to this night-time scene
Begging taxis to stop like some kind of fean
So, I could gather more for the Isolated drinking
Morning vodka for breakfast to stop me from overthinking
It's like every time I go home, I step into a version of my old
self, and I don't like it
How many times was I so wasted I wouldn't of know if my
drink someone had spiked it?
It's the loud voices and basic manners that go out the window
That leaves my voice almost in limbo
Because I know logically there is no point reasoning with
someone in a state
So, it shouldn't be up for debate
Just breathe in and out, in and out
Pretend you can't hear the crowd's shout!
You once loved Thursday, Friday, Saturday raving; they are just
having fun
Ye, but I couldn't stop when rose the sun
So, all the laughs and teenage early 20s pre drinks raving, and
then afters

Spiralled into apocalypse-like disasters
So, I don't want to see night-time Broad Street or the German
Market stalls
Because I can re-gather triggers from them all
That doesn't mean I begrudge others that do because that's not
the case
It's just when night-time falls in my home is where I feel safe
Some may call it being a recluse
Let your hair down have fun; you can still not drink and let
loose
It's not about drinking. It's what drinking to me represents
A box underground with no air vents
Is how I feel when I'm surrounded by it, smell it, or see it on
TV
That's not a you problem. It's solely on me
That's why there has to be
Boundaries
No, yes ticked on RSVPs to parties
I'll go to a spa and a coffee though I will wish you well and
send a card
It's your event and not about me, but I simply just find it too
hard
So don't take it personally if I or anyone like me has to say
Sorry, I can't come out to play; maybe next year, but I'm not
ready today...

Compete

I choose not to compete with anybody other than the yesterday
version of myself
Therefore, I only wish success upon anyone else
So, if you are keeping up with the Jones's to feel like you are
succeeding
You're cutting off your own nose to spite your face while they
are watching it bleeding
It's not my business how much money you make
Or that you are changed now after mistake after mistake
So, for the people who are trying to keep their heads above
water barely floating
Who sink each time they see others gloating
Concentrate on not watching but swimming
For those who say they are winning
Are losing because they need to take down others for that win
So, don't watch, just swim
Before you know it, you will be out of deep water
But don't swim to where the people are shallow
Just float with not against the tide
If you have something to hide
Set it free to the waves
For secrets enslave
The mind stops you from moving
Watch the waves take your worries; it is ever so soothing
I won't compete with you, for life is not a race
I will take on new goals at my own pace
So, if you are competing, you're already losing because you're
competing against someone who's not in
Not in it for the win
But to simply try to keep moving even on days when the tide is
rough, and arms are heavy
Moving slowly and steady
So, race against someone else if, like for I'm not in it for
winning
I'm just some days barely floating but continuing with my
swimming
I know something, though and I know it for sure

One day I'll find my way back to shore until the waves call me
again, and I go back for more
I only wish success upon anyone elsc
I am not competing against anybody but yesterday's version of
myself

Crinkles

She irons the pieces of her crumbled chest
She hangs them up and lets them rest
The creases fade and unwrinkled, so it would seem
She irons them again, this time using steam
For she knows it took many tumbles
To create so many crumbles
So just one iron will not do
She must persevere and push on through
She worries they may crease again so she covers them in magic
For she has found her way this time, so new lines would just
feel tragic
She smiles at strangers on the train
She sees their creases feels their pain
She tries to make polite conversation
Smiles with love when she leaves the station
For when a person has had creases upon their once whole chest
They see other's creases, and they wish them all the best
It might not just be heart pieces; sometimes it's your muddled
mind
Can feel like that lost sock in the laundry you just cannot find
Or the pile of clothes that are growing in the laundry basket
But we just apply makeup on our smile, because it's a really
good way to mask it
The creased heart the laundry pile does not have to feel so
much
If you just do a little every day to keep yourself in touch
With the daily routine and the weekly grind
One shirt at a time, one crease, one line, until finally, that lost
sock you find

Pebbles

You came to me in my dream last night. I think you have been
visiting for a while
This time it felt lighter your eyes seemed to smile
I think you have been sending me messages. I'm sorry it took
me so long to see
They were like Hansel and Gretel pebbles you left just for me
Little guides in the form of lighthouses, birds, and lessons not
what I wanted, but I did need
Because you knew even when I was hurting, I'd still fight on
and proceed
Don't be so trusting, and don't walk down country lanes on
your own
Don't let those spiritual vampires into your home
Protect yourself, and help others if you can, but not all see the
world in the same light
There is a reason you wake up in the middle of the night
'Oh, it's been you'
I get it now; there was something I needed to do
Somethings I needed to let go of somethings I needed to forget
You cleared the leaves upon my path, for they were filled with
regret
New leaves bring new promises, but old ones bring them too
It just means that they are falling to make way for something
new
Not all doors should be open with a universal key
Some are vaults keeping you from negative energy
Take notice of agendas, the sheep in wolf's clothing
Whose teeth show every now and again while they are secretly
loathing
But don't wish them any harm; it's a shame they are bitter
They cannot hear the Pitter patter, Patter Pitter
Of new beginnings, new energies, new moons, and new stars
But for those in your corner, close your eyes with me, for the
whole world is ours

227

Bed Snuggles

Last night my daughter and I got into bed, cuddled, and talked
all cosy and snug
Words feel much softer when intertwined with a hug.
She said to me this morning how she loves our chats and how
we make each other giggle
It made me forgive the midnight blanket stealing from her
continuous wiggles
She has her own bed, of course, but when it's cold and dark and
rainy outside
We just like to lie under the covers, lock the world out, and hide
Plus, she is like a human water bottle that always generates heat
I like it when it's all quiet, but I can feel the rhythms of her
little heartbeat
Sometimes we are in the same house, but in separate rooms,
then you have the routine, and the connection gets lost
With the dynamic of 'put your uniform on, listen to me, I'm the
boss'
So, it's nice to strip it all back to just her and I talking about
anything
Telling her that she is and always has been my everything
When they are in year six, it can feel like you are losing the
grasp of your child to the teenage world approaching
Hard to say those words out loud without that lump in your
throat choking
She won't always want to lie in bed with her mom talking about
her day
Her upset at not getting the role in the school play
There will be slammed doors, 'I hate you and oh that's not fair'
When I tell her to sort out her life and brush her hair
But I don't want to be having dramas about hairbrushes
I want to hear the playground gossip and her latest crushes
I want to be the one she turns to if she is sad or happy or not
sure what she feels
Because a mother's hug is soft, it heals
So, I'm going to hold on to the hugs in bed, conversations, and
I love you, Mommy moments for as long as I can get them.
Because they will only fly from the nest quicker if you let them

Daisy Chains

Let's sit and make some daisy chains, the pretty yellow and the
white
Let's place the crown upon our heads, pretend we are hippies
for the night
Let's make friendship bands made from flowers
Put them in our hair to pass the hours
Whenever I see daisies, it makes me want to make the chains
It takes me back to being a child, even daisies look sad when it
rains
In the sunshine though, they scatter the grass like pretty little
reminders of spring
A daisy chain, a daisy crown even a daisy ring
Little reminders that beauty is free
Scatted upon the grass for all to see
Little children play with daisies, the yellow and the white
I'm going to make a daisy chain and be a child again for the
night

Youth Work

Youth work no one day is the same
Then u have moments, when a quiet girl paints a picture of your face, and puts your name
Little things that are nods of acknowledgment, whether that be a fist pump, or a nod of the head
Mediation against fights, bubbling from the classic, he said she said
Challenging and frustrating, rewarding in so many ways
Whether that be hearing their poems, talking of their home life, or watching them create little plays
All it takes is one adult to believe in them, but trust takes a long time to build
Especially if home life is rocky, so they keep adults away with an aggressive shield
Why would they trust us though, if the very people who are supposed to love and care for them do not, not the way that they should
They get labelled naughty children, insolent, unapproachable a thug
Yet when you scratch the surface, and you open up a bit about your past
This shield melts like ice a little, then the conversations start to last
I tell them of my struggles with alcohol some (deffo not all) the things I got up to as a kid
I think communication should work that way, not just ask for all their information without willing to give
I see the young version of myself in them sometimes, and I just want to say please, please don't choose that route
Some of them walk round so full of anger, it's like they are a loaded gun just waiting to shoot
We have some Banta though, you deffo need to be able to handle a joke
Cuz sometimes your deep in the firing line, if u don't laugh it off then, you're likely to choke
You can't take things personal, I got called an ugly bowling ball head the other day

So, I just said if I'm a bowling ball, that makes u the pin, and
I'm rolling right your way
You need eyes in the back of your head, lucky I don't really
miss a trick
I've life experience to pull from, so I can reel them off they can
take their pick
That's why I called my company Been There Done That
So, u can hide behind makeup, or your balaclava and hat
I won't give up on you for swearing, wagging it, kicking off
making mistakes
Cuz to make it into recovery it took many breaks
So, I'm not in a position to judge others especially not the youth
You all have a place in my heart and when I say I'll help you
that's the truth
Youth work no one day is the same
Then you have moments when a quiet girl paints your face and
puts your name

CONSEQUENCE

Every time I see a post like this, it hurts my heart it makes me
cry
For a mothers lost her son, within the blink of an eye
She won't get to see him grow up, have kids or meet his wife
Because those moments were taken from a cold bladed knife
That smile she will not see on his graduation day
His eyes can't light up as he could watch his children play
For all the time he could have had has been taken away
Because another carried a knife that day
All the dreams he could have had things he could of achieved
Taken in blood as his mother grieves
And for what? for the perpetrator to sit his life away in a cell
Two mothers of two sons now life's a living hell
I see the faces of smiling lads come onto Posts for knife crime
I wish I had the power to freeze that smiling face, capture it in
time
So, the families and loved ones would not have to feel the pain
Of a life lost for foolishness, but a life not lost in vain
When I was younger if you had an issue, you would meet at the
school gate
A few punches here and there, shake it off, then gone was the
hate
Not one person I knew growing up, walked around with a
weapon in their pocket
Now it just seems the norm, I wish I had the power to stop it
How can the perpetrator not understand
That they will never wash away the blood on their hands
What punishment will be given to match this CONSEQUENCE
For now, a mother must talk of her Son, IN THE PAST TENSE

ARTHUR

Arthur you were loved, although not by the people you wanted
to be loved by
The picture of your little face has made a whole nation cry
Arthur you were loved, by people who didn't get the chance to
save you
You in your six years on this earth endured things an adult
hasn't gone through
You were loved and this whole country would have fed you, if
we were given the chance
Be a little boy in heaven now, climb trees, chase dreams, be a
superhero, dance
To this country you are a hero, you didn't need a fancy costume
The picture of you smiling could brighten up a room
You should have been able to smile more and learn, be loved
and play
Not stand facing a wall for 12 to 14 hours a day
In heaven there will be no walls just angels and their wings
You will sleep not on hard floors but clouds listening to angels
as they sing
Little beautiful boy you will have your round table for you have
the name of a king
All the angels will have gifts they shall bring
To make up for the days on this earth that you cried yourself to
sleep
You have brought grown men to tears for you and inside we
weep
You were loved, but the love you could have been given was
offered too late
But now angel Arthur you are protected behind the pearly gates

Happy Ending

You are my happy ending
Genuine, not just pretending
You are wise yet uncomplicated
A simple life underestimated
The things that we take for granted
Those positive seeds that you have planted
To help me grow, you can grow with me too
Love is not what you say, it's the things you do
I notice them, your kindness does not go a miss
I never knew a happiness that has felt like this
This is contentment
Without bitterness or resentment
Because we give each other space
I love your body and your face
Because your face is kind
Not a mask with agenda you hide behind
You make me feel at ease
Although you like to wind me up and like to tease
I know it's done in jest
Because you build me up to be the best
Version of myself
I've never had that from anyone else
So, it's strange but glorious
A partner that wishes you to be victorious
Instead of a mess
And yes
You make me laugh at the strangest of times
I make you listen to my latest Rhymes
You are the opposite of what I thought love felt like
You know the fireworks and all that hype
You are someone I want to grow old with
Even though you and Belle are a pair of divs
It's took time, but people are so quick to rush
I know I waffle on, and you probably think woman shush
But you are...
Genuine, not pretending
You are my happy ending

234

Through Isabella's Eyes

She does not have to stand at my funeral, wondering why she
wasn't enough
Having to face the world without mommy's love, this place is
already far too tough
She doesn't have to hide if she's been bullied, because she's
scared of how I will react
Mommies being irrational, heading to school with an axe
She doesn't have to watch me bottle watch when she just wants
to chill
She doesn't have to see me turning grey, as the poisons making
me ill
She does not have to live in chaos with a new drama every
week
Or do crazy things because it's attention that she seeks
She doesn't have to worry any more, that mommy's world is
upside down
Because she sees I'm stable now, with my feet firmly on the
ground
She doesn't have to act like the adult, while she is just a child
Mommies, having a duvet day again, I'm sure when she arises
the world will get wild
She doesn't have to worry, she doesn't have that weight
Of a mom who wakes up craving, and it's only half past eight
What she does get is....
Consistency
Accountability
Sustainability
Stability
The things a child needs the most
Not a vessel to the vodka, and Mommy is the host
She gets cuddles, she's always had them, but these mean so
much more
Mommies not craving cuddles, because her head is feeling sore
There is no question the loves always been there, because she's
always been my light
It's just I was battling an internal fight
She gets a home full of laughter

Not disaster
Clothes that smell like softener, floors far less sticky
A man in my life, who would never in a million years ever hit
me
She has a home life, school life, routine
A mother who finds positive solutions to young girls being
mean
Affirmations to build confidence, advice that makes more sense
Than 'smash her in the face belle and push her up the fence'
Don't get me wrong, even my sober mind says 'defend
yourself, and don't take any shit'
But I think now, before it all spits out like a dragon's flame fire
pit
She has her friend round we bake cookies, but I give her, her
own space
Mommy doesn't fall to sleep with last night's make up on her
face
We are a team
Living only what we could describe as a dream
That I never knew was possible, it came as a pleasant surprise
That as I got well, so did the view from Isabella's eyes

Places to go to for help and hope

Changes UK Addiction services 0121 769 1000

St Basils Help for young homeless people ages 16 -25
0121 772 2483

National Domestic Abuse Helpline – 0808 2000 247 –
www.nationaldahelpline.org.uk/

The Men's Advice Line, for male domestic abuse survivors –
0808 801 0327 (run by Respect)

The Mix, free information and support for under 25s in the UK
– 0808 808 4994

National LGBT+ Domestic Abuse Helpline – 0800 999 5428
(run by Galop)

We Are with You provide free and confidential support to
people experiencing issues with drugs, alcohol or mental health.

Al-anon Al-Anon provides support to anyone affected by
someone else's drinking (Alcohol Concern0 National agency on
alcohol misuse

FRANK Information, support and counselling for drug users and
their families.

rehab4addiction A free helpline for those affected by substance
misuse run by people who've beaten drug and alcohol rehab
themselves

Domestic Abuse, Sexual Violence and Substance Use Online
service providing advice and support for substance use, domestic
abuse and sexual violence

National Youth Advocacy Service Information and advocacy
service for children and young people up to 24 years.

Childnet Childnet Hub is for young people aged 11-18, you'll find top tips, competitions, blogs and advice to help you to use the internet safely, responsibly and positively.

Action for Children Support for vulnerable and neglected children and young people, and their families

Shelter The UK's largest housing charity gives information on housing rights, homelessness and state benefits.

Your local Citizens' Advice Bureau (CAB) provides free, confidential and independent advice, including advice on housing. The website has information in Welsh, Bengali, Chinese, Gujarati, Punjabi and Urdu, as well as English, and allows you to locate your nearest CAB (www.citizensadvice.org.uk)

Shelter Homelessness due to domestic violence If you have to leave your home because of threats, abuse or intimidation, there may be safe places you can go to, such as refuges and temporary housing from the council. It may also be possible to stay in your home and make it safer.

Claiming homelessness – Under current law you can approach any Homeless Persons Unit if it is unsafe for you to remain in your home due to domestic violence. The Council is obliged to offer you temporary accommodation while they carry out their assessment or give you a decision on your application on the day. Housing law states that, 'It is not reasonable for a person to continue to occupy accommodation if it is probable that this will lead to domestic violence or other violence'. Violence means violence or threats of violence from another person, which are likely to be carried out.

Rethink The largest severe mental illness charity in the UK

Mind Information and support on mental health issues, including how to get help.

National Self Harm Network A forum for survivors, professionals and family

Fast Forward Information on drugs and alcohol education for youth.

Bursting the Bubble Website for teenagers living with family violence.

Open Dorz
Emily Ashmore (who also works at Newman university and is a close friend of mine who works wonders)
https://www.letsopendorz.com

Newman University
Newman is a university that has help many people overcome their social, emotional and mental barriers and creates a safe environment for people to thrive.

Sifa Fire Side
Welcome to SIFA Fireside. Drop in Centre where people can get help, I talk about Sifa in the Homeless chapter.

Fircroft College
Address: 1018 Bristol Road, Birmingham B29 6LH
Phone: 0121 472 0116
Hours: Open · Closes 17:00
Age range: 19 - 99
School type: Further Education
Education Phase: Senior
Local authority: Birmingham
Gender: Mixed
Admission policy: Non selective
Email: admissions@fircroft.ac.uk

The Childrens Society The Children's Society | UK children's charity childrenssociety.org.uk

If you are struggling with the cost of living, then your local council have a pot of funding specifically for this. Called **the welfare provision fund**, you can also get help with council tax reduction etc here. Your local councils website it a great place to start should you want to find information of local organisations in your area. Each council will have a living well section which will have a data base of providers who may be able to help you.

Know your rights
The gingerbread website can help you.
0808 802 0925
www.gingerbread.org.uk

Samaritans
0330 094 5717
https://www.samaritans.org/

Prevent Suicide
www.nspa.org.uk.

Support after Suicide Partnership
www.mentalhealth.org.uk

Find a Meeting | Alcoholics Anonymous - Great Britain (alcoholics-anonymous.org.uk)

Welcome | UKNA Meetings | Narcotics Anonymous Meetings in the United Kingdom

Self-Help Addiction Recovery | UK Smart Recovery

With the world we live in today there is a wealth of knowledge at the click of a button no not be afraid to ask google. Go to your local library or support groups.

Never be afraid to ask for help, it doesn't make you less of a person. It is far braver to admit you are struggling than mask through your pain.

Ingram Content Group UK Ltd.
Milton Keynes UK
UKHW020639230523
422205UK00014B/420